PRAISE FOR

DON'T PICK UP ALL THE DOG HAIRS

"Ron has been a visionary leader in one of the great successes in our US healthcare system, the community health center movement, for over 30 years. Over nearly 20 of those years, I have known and found Ron to be a dedicated, humble, and innovative leader with a wonderful sense of humor. It is so exciting to see his learnings, lessons, and teachings in this book in 30+ accessible and motivating chapters. This book is like having Ron at your side quietly telling you what not to do with the brilliant insights and entertaining style that are uniquely his. Thank you, Ron for sharing and inspiring us with your commitment, caring, and endearing wit!"

—**Kyu Rhee,** MD, MPP, Senior Vice President
and Chief Medical Officer, CVS Health;
and Chief Medical Officer, Aetna

"Ron Dwinnells is a leader and role model. His gentle wisdom, warm sense of humor, and true humility shine through every line of this valuable set of learnings and teachings about leadership."

—**Ellen L. Beck,** MD, Faculty Director of Faculty and
Leadership Development and Clinical Professor,
Department of Family Medicine and Public Health,
University of California, San Diego School of Medicine

"I have known Dr. Ronald Dwinnells for over 30 years. We have worked together on multiple levels and in multiple venues. I have observed him over these many years as he has blossomed into an outstanding and revered leader in the healthcare industry and a blessing to underserved communities. Therefore, I can attest to the truth of his warm and insightful narrative on leadership principles. He walks the talk, and people listen. His lessons on leadership F-A-M-E are easily digestible and instructive on how to navigate and negotiate one's journey of leadership. Ron speaks directly to those who intend for their journey to lead to personal fulfillment and sustainability of those who would follow."

—**Walter J. Clark, Jr.,** MD, MSHCM, FASAM,
Vice President, Primary Care Service Line,
VA Pittsburgh Healthcare System

"Dr. Dwinnells has won our Outstanding MPH Community Faculty Award more times than any faculty in the program—with great reason. His stories and case examples on leadership are the highlight of the class, and I have heard students practicing what he has discussed in class—one student had one of his sayings posted on her wall during her doctoral program! I have heard Dr. Dwinnells teach year after year and never get tired of his creative approach and stories!"

—**Amy Lee,** MD, MPH, MBA, Professor and Program Director,
Consortium of Eastern Ohio, Master of Public Health,
Northeast Ohio Medical University

"I enjoyed the life lessons shared by Ron in *Don't Pick Up All the Dog Hairs*. Dr. Dwinnells's distinctive anecdotes told from his relatable perspective are both amusing and edifying. He reminds us that our failures are one of the most important stepping-stones to our success. His tales of what not to do constructed from his own experiences in leadership roles offer an insightful and entertaining guide. I am proud to call Ron a friend and leader in our community."

—**Edward W. Muransky,** CEO, The Muransky Companies

"In *Don't Pick Up All the Dog Hairs*, Dr. Ronald Dwinnells, a highly respected healthcare professional, shares lessons learned from his many years of management experience in a fun and compelling must-read. Incorporating humor and examples, the author makes it easy for the reader to remember and apply the lessons to a variety of situations and improve his or her management skills."

—**Renee W. Dean,** Renee W. Dean Health Care Consulting

"Every leader will gain significant insight while enjoying Dr. Dwinnells' *Don't Pick Up All the Dog Hairs*. The format is perfect for the busy professional, and the wisdom is extraordinary. A must-read for those seeking to be a servant leader."

—**James P. Tressel,** President, Youngstown State University

DON'T PICK UP ALL *the* DOG HAIRS

RONALD DWINNELLS, MD, MBA

DON'T PICK UP ALL *the* DOG HAIRS

Lessons *for* Life & Leadership

Illustrations by Daria Sansoterra

GREENLEAF
BOOK GROUP PRESS

Published by Greenleaf Book Group Press
Austin, Texas
www.gbgpress.com

Distributed by Greenleaf Book Group

For ordering information or special discounts for bulk purchases, please contact Greenleaf Book Group at PO Box 91869, Austin, TX 78709, 512.891.6100.

Design and composition by Greenleaf Book Group and Teresa Muniz
Cover design by Greenleaf Book Group and Teresa Muniz
Cover images used under license from ©Shutterstock.com/Eric Isselee, ©Shutterstock.com/Feng Yu. Bone icon from ©The Noun Project/Adrien Coquet
Illustrations by Daria Sansoterra

Publisher's Cataloging-in-Publication data is available.

Print ISBN: 978-1-62634-869-1

eBook ISBN: 978-1-62634-870-7

Part of the Tree Neutral® program, which offsets the number of trees consumed in the production and printing of this book by taking proactive steps, such as planting trees in direct proportion to the number of trees used: www.treeneutral.com

TreeNeutral®

Printed in the United States of America on acid-free paper

21 22 23 24 25 26 10 9 8 7 6 5 4 3 2 1

First Edition

This book is lovingly dedicated to my parents, Hisako Yoshikawa Dwinnells, who had the will and courage to survive Allied bombings of her Japanese homeland during World War II, and Donald Arthur Dwinnells, retired US Army serviceman who fought to defend his country in World War II and the Korean conflict. They bestowed life, love, and the means to overcome adversities.

It is also dedicated to my in-laws, John N. Cernica, PhD, an internationally renowned civil engineer and university professor, who gave the gift of knowledge to students throughout the world, and Patricia Marinelli Cernica, who imparted spiritual wisdom to my life.

Finally, I dedicate this book to my wife, Kathy, who gave her full encouragement and devotion to me and this endeavor.

Their inspiration helped fulfill my dreams and passions.

Errare humanum est,
perseverare diabolicum.

Meaning: To err is human,
to persist in it is diabolical!

CONTENTS

FOREWORD

I'm a former NASA astronaut. When I was still working for NASA, I bumped into Ron Dwinnells while we were both working out in a hotel in Cape Canaveral, Florida. My job took me to Cape Canaveral many times, including twice to launch on Space Shuttle missions, but this time I was there with my family to get on a cruise ship for a vacation (many traveling adventures start in Cape Canaveral!). Ron and I happened to be heading off on the same cruise. We hit it off and have been friends ever since. We have even shared leadership stories a time or two. In this book, Ron shares how failure, adversity, and mistakes create excellent lessons for life and leadership, and it made me reflect on my own life and how I navigated my own trials and tribulations.

I grew up in Wadsworth, Ohio. When I was about eight years old (in 1965), I started hearing about astronauts. Several of the original US astronauts—namely, John Glenn, Neil Armstrong, and Jim Lovell (think Tom Hanks from the movie *Apollo 13*)—were from Ohio. The news media talked and wrote about their exploits on TV and in the newspapers. I heard about them and thought that being an astronaut and exploring space sounded like a great job. I wanted to find out more about them, so I obtained a copy of the book that the original seven US astronauts wrote: *We Seven*. One thing I learned was that four out of the seven original astronauts had been naval aviators (a pilot in either the US Navy or the Marine Corps). I was hooked on the idea of becoming an astronaut and decided that I would be a US Navy pilot and then move on to NASA.

When I told my parents my plan, my dad told me that if I was thinking about becoming a US Navy pilot, I should find out about a school called the US Naval Academy. I asked him what this school was, but he told me to find out for myself; he wanted me to do the research, just as I had researched the original astronauts.

Of course, we didn't have computers back then, so I didn't have access to Google. Instead, I wrote a letter to the US Naval Academy and asked them to send me some information about their school. They sent me a colorful catalog that showed students at the academy playing every sport you can imagine—baseball, basketball, football, soccer, swimming, track and field. They showed students playing sports I had never even heard of, like rugby, lacrosse, and fencing. They didn't have a lot of pictures of students sitting in class studying, but I found out later that that's what college students do a lot of! Anyway, I saw all those sports activities and told my dad, "This looks like summer camp! Sign me up for the Naval Academy!"

I soon found out that you must have very good grades in high school to get into the academy, so I started studying hard. One of my early life lessons was that if I put in the time and effort, I could achieve difficult things. My hard work in school paid off, and I was accepted. When I first arrived at the academy, they asked me what subject I wanted to major in during my college career. I told them I liked math and science the best and thought I wanted to study engineering. They told me that the Naval Academy had many types of engineering available for study—mechanical, electrical, systems, computer, ocean (this was the *Naval* Academy, after all), aerospace. When I heard *aerospace engineering*, I said, "Wait! I want to be an astronaut. I think I should study aero*space* engineering," and so I did.

Four years later, I graduated from the Naval Academy and was commissioned an officer in the US Navy. Since I wanted to be a pilot, the

US Navy sent me to flight training, and I earned my wings of gold as a naval aviator.

I loved flying. Early in my career, I found out that if I wanted to be an astronaut, I should become a test pilot, because NASA liked to select astronauts from the ranks of military test pilots. I applied to the US Naval Test Pilot School and was told after applying that I had been selected as an alternate to the next class.

That sounded good, so I asked what it meant to be an alternate. I was told that they select primary candidates and alternates for each class. Being a student at the test pilot school requires a pilot to be able to fly part of the day and go to class part of the day, so if a student falls down the stairs and breaks a leg and can't fly for two or three months, they move that student back to a later class and call one of the alternates to take his place. Unfortunately for me, nobody fell down and broke a leg, so I did not get to attend that class. The good thing was that they had a new class starting every six months, so I immediately applied again, but I did not get selected on my second attempt.

At the same time, I needed to move to a new US Navy job, and I received a call from someone in Washington, DC, telling me that they had a slot for me, if I was interested, to attend the US Naval Postgraduate School and get a master's degree in aeronautical engineering. When I heard this, I thought, "More college? College is hard! I don't really want to go back to school!" but that person calling me was very persistent and told me that getting a master's degree would help me get accepted into test pilot school and maybe even become an astronaut. He twisted my arm, and I agreed to go back to school. It turned out to be the best decision I made in my career. I know I would not be an astronaut today if I didn't have that master's degree in aeronautical engineering. I moved my family to Monterey, California, and started my graduate work.

As I began my studies, I thought it was time to start my application to the astronaut program. I knew that if I wanted to be an astronaut, I would have to eventually apply; they were not going to just come knock on my door and say, "Mike, do you want to be an astronaut?" I needed to fill out an application and send it to NASA.

In the meantime, I was continuing to apply to the US Naval Test Pilot School every chance I could. The third time I applied, nothing. The fourth time I applied, nothing. Finally, I asked them, "Why, after being an alternate the first time, have I not been selected as a primary candidate in my next applications?" They told me that every class was different, with different pilot needs, and I just needed to keep trying.

Meanwhile, I never heard back from NASA after my first astronaut application was submitted. I was not dismayed by that. After all, I knew that I didn't have my master's degree yet, and I hadn't been to test pilot school either—two things I thought were important before NASA would consider me seriously. All the rejections from the test pilot school were preparing me for the NASA rejection. Unfortunately, the NASA application process at that time was on a two-year cycle, so I had to wait two years before I could apply again. In the meantime, I continued working and graduated with my master's.

The US Navy then sent me to a ship. I had joined the US Navy to fly airplanes and become an astronaut, not to go on a ship! But orders are orders, and I went to the USS *Coral Sea* for two and a half years. While serving on the *Coral Sea*, I continued to apply to the US Naval Test Pilot School and to NASA. On my eighth application to the test pilot school, I was finally accepted and moved to Patuxent River, Maryland, to start my year as a test pilot student.

After graduating from the Naval Test Pilot School, they sent me to a squadron. It was great; if you like flying airplanes, you will love being a test pilot. I flew jets, helicopters, gliders, a Soviet MiG-21, Brazilian experimental jets, and more. After 10 months, the Naval Test Pilot School asked me to come back to be an instructor. I said, "Wait a minute. I applied to your school eight times before I was selected, and now after being a test pilot for only 10 months, you want me to be an instructor?" They told me that things like that happen sometimes. They said that I had done well as a student, and they thought I would be a good instructor. I took them up on their offer.

Being an instructor at the test pilot school was the second-best job I've ever had. On any given day, I might be flying a glider in the morning and an F-18 fighter jet in the afternoon. I loved it, but I still wanted to be an astronaut, so every two years, I continued to send in my NASA application. I didn't hear anything from NASA after my second, third, fourth, fifth, or sixth applications. Then it was time to change jobs again, and the US Navy sent me to a desk in Washington, DC. No planes to fly—ouch!

I thought my chances of becoming an astronaut were probably about zero, but I submitted my seventh NASA application in 1995. I was in a meeting in Washington when the phone rang and a woman at the Johnson Space Center in Houston asked me if I was interested in coming down for an interview. I was thrilled! I went to Houston and spent an entire week there so I could undergo every medical test they could think of. Then, for 45 minutes during that week, I went into a room for my first job interview ever.

I had been a newspaper delivery boy, I'd been a busboy in a restaurant, and I had painted bridges and guardrails on the roads around Wadsworth. But these were all jobs that did not involve interviews. You filled out an application and put your phone number on it, and if they wanted to hire you, they just called. Then I went to the US Naval Academy. If you graduate from a service academy in the United States, you don't have to interview for your first job. They hand you a diploma and a set of orders, and off you go.

So I walked into my first job interview at NASA, and there were 12 people in that room to ask me questions. It was a little intimidating at first, but they were asking about me, and I figured that I knew more about me than anyone else in the room, so I relaxed and tried to just have fun talking to them. Some of the questions were a little tough, though, like when an Air Force Academy graduate astronaut asked me why I went to the Naval Academy instead of the Air Force Academy! I explained that I had read *We Seven* and set my course based on what I had learned from that book. Of course, the Air Force Academy wasn't even established yet when the original seven astronauts were in school, so none of them could have gone there.

I waited nine months from the time I interviewed until NASA made their selections for the astronaut class of 1996. They called me and told me I had not been selected. This was a bad day. I had worked hard, I had done everything that I thought I needed to do, but it wasn't good enough.

But I had a dream to become an astronaut and fly in space, so I continued to work toward that goal. I set my sights on the next application cycle and reapplied. I got the same phone call from Houston and was invited to again go through the astronaut interview process. When I arrived in Houston the second time, I asked the medical staff if I had to redo all the medical tests since I had just done them two years before. The NASA doctors said I had to do all the tests again; even the proctologist was nodding. I did all the tests and went back to the same room for my interview. A lot of the same 12 people were in that room again to interview me. Some of the questions were even tougher this time, like when astronaut Bob Cabana said, "Mike, we didn't select you two years ago. Why should we select you this time?" That was tough, especially since this was just my second job interview ever!

Again, I had to wait about nine months for NASA to make their decision. This time I was selected into the program. I had been inspired by astronauts in NASA's first and second groups, and in 1998, I was selected into their 17th group of astronauts.

After having been a naval officer, a test pilot, and an astronaut, I'm currently the mayor of Friendswood, Texas. I am often asked to share my thoughts on leadership with various business groups, corporate leaders, and others. One of my slides on leadership says, "Forget your mistakes," because, as an astronaut, I learned it is critical to the success of the space mission that if and when I make a mistake, I have to quickly put that behind me and focus on the next task I am faced with. My good friend Dr. Dwinnells, on the other hand, has made a career of remembering his mistakes and learning from them! That is what makes this book such an important read for current and future leaders. Learn from Ron's mistakes instead of reinventing the wheel and making them yourself!

—Michael J. Foreman
Captain, US Navy (ret),
Former NASA astronaut

INTRODUCTION

"Maybe I can talk of my mistakes and
awkward stumbles. Maybe I can assure
the young that wisdom is the daughter of
failure yet the mother of success."

—Fay Vincent

Leadership is more an art than a science. Art involves fluidity and gaiety of life, like emotions, feelings, thoughts, and ideas, whereas science is things like precision, carrying out tasks, and planning. Since much of leadership deals with people and their emotions and getting them to do things, a leader needs to be in touch with the art side of life. They must know how to affect the emotional side of people.

My first foray into the art of leadership was a blur. After I was elected as president of my fourth-grade class in 1964, the only action I knew to take was to look important while wandering aimlessly on the recess playground. My friends became self-appointed "bodyguards" and were constant companions. They always wore dark sunglasses, even on cloudy days, making them appear malevolent. The heightened national security at the time (President Kennedy had been shot only a few months earlier) made everyone cautious, so my protectors carried and occasionally fired "finger guns" concealed in their pants pockets.

Although I did enjoy being the class president, I later discovered my true passion in the field of medicine. After completing medical school and a three-year pediatric residency training, I wrote a grant and helped start a small safety-net clinic to serve the poor. I became its first medical director and a physician who no longer had to pretend to be a leader like I did in the fourth grade. As a physician, I knew exactly what to do. I understood what made people tick and what made them sick. I could fix ailments, save lives, and even teach people how to stay healthy. My analytical abilities were spot-on; I had seven years of formal education beyond college, extensive training, and even some FAME (failure, adversity, mistakes, and enemies). Little did I know how important experiences—especially bad ones—completed my education.

Being the clinic's medical director—a "boss" title—was an entirely different experience. My duty was to tell people what to do, make up rules, and come up with efficient and effective ways to operate the clinic's day-to-day activities. In school, I never learned how to get people to do things. I do recall trying to learn how to be a leader by reading books and articles on leadership, but most everything portrayed idealism. It all felt unattainable, unrealistic. I soon realized I was on my own trying to understand the art of leadership. Rather, these skills are learned through experiences and mistakes, not some dusty old textbooks.

Leadership and life are full of roadblocks, but we can learn from real-life anecdotes of bad experiences that many of us have encountered. We learn and understand what not to do from our own mistakes, as well as those of others.

FOUR LEADERSHIP TRAITS

Over many years as a leader, I concluded there are four essential characteristics a person must possess to be a good leader. They conveniently fit into two categories: head and heart.

The head

The head category has to do with concrete and abstract thoughts, problem-solving, and knowledge application.

An important first leadership trait is analytical ability—the skill sets and tools that leaders have learned or acquired from studying and performing tasks. For example, an engineer labors over complicated formulas, then uses the information to build a bridge. We have all learned specific skill sets to help make us experts at our chosen profession.

It also involves cognition, a second essential trait. An effective leader must possess the fundamental capabilities to be perceptive and able to think through and solve problems. Much of this is a function of education (formally derived skill sets) and experiences (informally derived skill sets through on-the-job training). Interestingly, some people have this type of cognition built in. Somehow, they are born with an innate ability to think well, despite minimal education or experience. The reverse is also true: There are those who have multiple college degrees but have absolutely no ability to think logically.

The heart

The heart category is all about the intangible aspect of doing things—the feel of whether it is right or wrong and how to get people to do things.

A third trait involves the leader's emotional intelligence abilities. Being logical, smart, and having lots of experiences are not enough to be a great leader. To be the best, we must also possess other types of intelligence, such as understanding how people feel and harnessing those emotions for good. Leaders must be able to communicate in a way that makes people do what they want them to do while keeping them happy and effective. For example, it is far better, kinder, and gentler to ask, "Could you please help me out and do this for me? That would be so kind of you," than to forcefully command, "I TOLD YOU TO GO DO THAT!" As the saying goes, "You catch more flies with honey than with vinegar." This illustrates communication ability, self-regulation (controlling your behavior), self-awareness (knowing that you should ask nicely), and social skills—key components for emotional intelligence. These qualities are the glue that helps bring the head and the heart together. Without emotional intelligence, leadership would be severely weakened.

The heart also requires a fourth trait: the gut instinct. Early on, I learned to go with my gut in most decision-making, goal-setting, and people-managing experiences. After all, the gut is the same as instinct, and it is a culmination of the previous three characteristics. There are times when you just don't know why or how you get answers, but you just go with your gut, and it is usually correct. Consider this quote about love from Blaise Pascal: "The heart has its reasons which reason knows not."

The underlying foundation to these four traits is the element of time, which provides experiences. Experiences help hone the important skills of leadership. Therefore, most high-level executive jobs require people to have years of experiences before they can be hired. Remember, you cannot plant seeds in September and expect a crop by October.

Be assured, these four elements will eventually blend in, and one day, as a seasoned leader, you will discover that your gut instinct will take over most decision-making. You will simply know what to do.

LET'S TALK ABOUT FAME

Charlie was no friend of mine. This cute Labrador retriever was a tormentor and a cunning foe who harassed me from the day he arrived. Loud, lewd, large, and smelly, his body emitted such an odor that it often brought a wrinkle to my nose and tears to my eyes. Even worse, he frequently plopped his horizontal, four-foot-one-inch-long, 138-pound body anywhere and everywhere, causing me to alter my walking patterns to avoid tripping. The ceramic kitchen floor was often wet from drool and urine, making it as slippery as a winter ice rink.

The absolute worst thing about Charlie was his hair. Billions and billions of short, blond, and coarse hairs, with invisible mites and dander hitching rides on every single strand. They seemed to magnify and become intensely more visible when sunlight beamed through the windows, effectively exposing every strand floating, then coming to a rest deep in the carpet fibers.

My goal was to oust him. "He should be an outside dog," I declared to my family. He should shed hair, drool, and urine in a natural, outdoor setting like animals should. Despite my best efforts to banish him from the interior of my house, I failed.

Although the futility of my quest was annoying, I am grateful for the important life and leadership lessons he taught me. As he grew older, we became pals—morning walks after his dose of insulin, followed by a hearty breakfast. He has passed now, but Charlie's story illustrates that failing (my failure to banish him to the great outdoors) is sometimes good for us. It adds color to our lives, builds integrity, forges resilience, and—best of all—instills wisdom. These are all essential elements for leadership excellence and a successful life.

Curiously, many people have difficulty learning from mistakes and adversity. It begs the question, *Why are we so resistant to learn from our less-than-successful attempts at things?*

Life and leadership lessons can often be illustrated through failure, adversity, mistakes, and even enemies—what I commonly refer to as "FAME." Difficult experiences teach lessons that make us wiser so that we may avoid similar obstacles in the future. Only if we recognize, embrace, and learn from adversity will it serve us well and lead to positive outcomes.

Mistakes are as important to leadership as spices are to foods. A spice alone is not tasty but is rather pungent. When added to certain foods, the flavors are enhanced and often become indescribably delicious. Likewise, leaders without negative experiences are usually bland and will most likely be ineffective, while those who experienced innumerable losses will likely become the great ones.

Like many in positions of great responsibility, I made a lot of mistakes during my 40-year career as a doctor, researcher, teacher, and health-care administrator. I made even more in my personal life as a son, husband, and father. During my early childhood, I made a lot of "dumb" mistakes but often acted as if they never happened. I was like the cartoon ostrich, sticking my head in a hole and pretending everything was okay—out of sight, out of mind. Why did I do that? I'm not sure, but it was probably because of embarrassment and the feeling of inadequacy. Psychologists call this *repression*—a defense adjustment mechanism. But please don't do that! It is good to make mistakes and acknowledge them; they are such valuable life lessons.

The principles of life and leadership can be learned through stories of FAME; they are opportunities to learn and improve our leadership skills. Encountering these four challenges can kindle self-analysis, enhancing awareness of what went wrong and what not to do in the future.

In Fay Vincent's excellent editorial in the *Wall Street Journal* (Saturday/Sunday, July 20-21, 2019) titled "A Good Life in My Dying Days," he suggests bestowing the wisdoms acquired through mistakes and difficulties to the younger generation.

Not only do these experiences render life and leadership lessons, but so do interactions with people. Most relationships with others are positive, and we can learn from them; however, those who create trouble through passive-aggressive tendencies, speak badly of you, or spread false information to undermine you or your efforts can also be a valuable education. Although the word *enemies* seems ominous, the reality is that the people we interact with daily may later emerge as antagonists. Individuals can become jealous of your power or influence; they want to take things away from you or perhaps will not agree with certain issues or decisions. This is very real and an integral part of leadership, just like death is a part of life. Don't shy away from those who hurt you. You can learn from those adversaries!

FAME is a set of tools that teaches us *what not to do*, both in leadership and in life. Other tools, such as emotional intelligence, gut instincts, and analytical abilities, help us navigate and better understand our role as leaders. We can also develop principles that are applied to everyday life situations based on what we learn. Good ideas and advice often evolve from negative experiences.

Certainly, there are no well-defined algorithms or templates for leadership behavior and decision-making, and this is not a scientific or academic book on leadership. Every situation is unique, but the principles remain relatively constant. I have not tested anything through scientific methods; rather, they were tested in the school of hard knocks.

Together, we'll ignite awareness, and I'll relate difficult situations that you may have already experienced. It is by no means a way to teach anyone how to act or how to be. If you are a novice leader with little to no experience, then this collection of anecdotes and observations is a heads-up on things that happen in the real world and how you may be able to deal with them.

When we screwed up as kids, some of us didn't listen to our mom as she wagged her index finger, exclaiming, "Don't do that!" If only we had listened! Now, we have to learn from our own FAME to know what not to do.

Food for thought

To be a great leader, we must experience and learn from failure, adversity, and mistakes and must even acquire a few enemies along the way. Using analytical skills, cognitive abilities, emotional intelligence, and gut instincts to learn from these adverse experiences is the key to great leadership and can serve us well in all aspects of life. What failures have you experienced in life, and did you learn anything from them?

CHAPTER 1

DON'T LIVE IN A FISHBOWL

"Laughter is timeless, imagination
has no age, dreams are forever."

—Walt Disney

The Walt Disney Company was founded in 1923. By 2017, it owned eleven theme parks, two water parks, and several television networks, including ABC (the American Broadcasting Company). Remarkably, Walter Elias Disney and his brother Roy O. Disney began their empire with $40 and a small cartoon studio located in their uncle Robert's garage. Known as a great visionary, innovator, and a world-class dreamer, Walt Disney and his most famous character, Mickey Mouse, soon became household names, launching entertainment and other forms of enjoyment for decades. His motto—dream, believe, dare, and do—along with strong-willed determination, courage, and a belief in his own abilities were the ingredients of his success.

Another futurist and visionary was Buckminster Fuller, the designer of the geodesic dome. He was also an unconventional thinker with no limitations. He published more than 30 books, coining or popularizing terms such as *Spaceship Earth*; *Dymaxion*, a word he made up, consisting of *dynamic*, *maximum*, and *tension*, to describe his futuristic vision of cars and houses; and *ephemeralization*, a term he used to describe the concept of using less material for greater results, such as for housing and his geodesic domes.[1]

These two men are examples of many throughout history who saw life's opportunities differently than most. They explored imagination, dreams, and fantasies to make the impossible achievable. Their visions had no boundaries, while their minds were like factories that produced realities.

DREAMS, IMAGINATION, AND FANTASIES

Dreams are what inspiration can become, imagination is the ability to see visions into the future, and fantasies make the impossible happen. They are the true essence of life and living. Applying them to the real world is what makes life greater; they help create a more fulfilling future. Performing seemingly impossible tasks is part of what makes leadership fun. Imagination is one of the most powerful tools a human being can possess. Imagination allowed us to go to the moon and to plan to go to Mars and beyond. It permits us to look deep into space and see past limitations.

Often, leaders must use these whimsical tools in order to solve problems, plan new projects, and improve their organizations. A good and effective leader must think outside the box. We need to look for opportunities to be imaginative. We are visionaries, and if you never leave your comfort zone, then how will you grow and expand your horizons?

THINKING OUTSIDE THE BOX

During World War II, military officers investigated how they could better protect airplanes and their crew. After studying and analyzing the bullet holes suffered during missions, they discovered specific patterns of areas the planes seemed to be hit the most. Looking for opportunities for efficiency and hoping to reduce mortalities, they centered their interest on moving the airplane's armor from areas in which there was a lower probability of getting shot to the more vulnerable parts of the plane. They reasoned that you could get the same protection with less armor if you concentrate the armor on the areas where the planes were getting hit the most.

They presented the following data[2] to Abraham Wald, a professor of mathematics at Columbia University and a member of the Statistical Research Group,[3] and posed the question of exactly how much more armor should belong on those vulnerable parts of the plane.

Section of plane	Bullet holes per square foot
Engine	1.11
Fuselage	1.73
Fuel system	1.55
Rest of the plane	1.8

Figure 1.1.

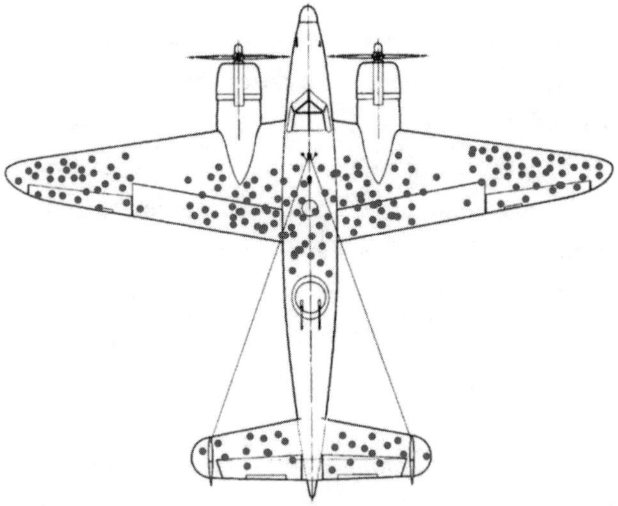

Figure 1.2.

Wald's reply was "Gentlemen, you need to put more armor plates where the holes aren't because that's where the holes were on the airplanes that didn't return!"[4]

Abraham Wald had the ability to think differently. To think outside the box means to think in a different way, from an unconventional perspective. The most successful people, including leaders, accomplish this because they do not limit themselves. Curiosity is an incredible characteristic that connects dreams to reality.

CAN CREATIVITY, IMAGINATION, FANTASY, AND DREAMS BE TAUGHT?

Is it possible to get people to be more imaginative and creative, to have visions of the future, or to think outside the box? According to Rom Schrift, a marketing professor at the University of Pennsylvania's Wharton School, "There are individual differences in our propensity to be creative. If you train yourself—and there are different methods for doing this—you can become more creative. There are individual differences in people, but I would argue that it is also something that can be developed and, therefore, taught."[5] Furthermore, another Wharton professor, Jerry (Yoram) Wind, who taught a creativity course at Wharton, says, "In any population, basically, the distribution of creativity follows the normal curve. At the absolute extreme, you have Einstein and Picasso, and you don't have to teach them; they are geniuses. Nearly everyone else in the distribution—and the type of people you would deal with at leading universities and companies—can learn creativity."[6]

Jennifer Mueller, a management professor at the University of San Diego, indicates that creativity may be a function of the environment. She believes that creativity can be shut off—or turned on—if the environment supports creativity.[7]

This may very well be true, as exemplified by John Denver's writing of "Annie's Song" on a ski lift ride to the top of Ajax Mountain, in Aspen, Colorado. He and his wife, Annie, were having difficulties, and after a reconciliation, he was suddenly inspired to write the lyrics by the time the ride reached the top.[8] He was inspired by a difficult event that stimulated his creativity.

It seems that some people do different things to help themselves be more creative. I am not aware of any specific exercises or strategies to improve this, but, often and unintentionally, I am able to see shapes, faces, animals, buildings, and other images when looking at clouds, wallpaper patterns, and wood grains. This gets my imagination going, and sometimes it stimulates me to think of things outside the box. This process of seeing things in certain patterns is called *pareidolia*, the tendency for incorrect perception of a stimulus as an object, pattern, or meaning known to the observer, such as seeing shapes in clouds, seeing faces in inanimate objects or abstract patters, and hearing hidden messages in music.[9] Perhaps this is an exercise we can engage in to help stimulate our imaginative powers, stimulate our creative juices, or see things beyond convention.

Another method to stimulate different thinking patterns is to consider choosing educational classes in something you are completely unfamiliar with. This is a great way to think about something differently. For example, in college, my major was biology, but I took a few classes in Latin, music appreciation, and art. They gave me a different perspective on how to look at problems from different angles.

Another way I have learned to think differently is to do completely unrelated things from the problems I may be contemplating. Mowing the lawn or cleaning the house, even building things, always puts me in a different mode of thinking.

Sometimes, unorthodox rituals help outstanding leaders think or do things differently. For example, Richard Branson, founder of Virgin Group, sparks his creativity by moving. "I find that I often come up with my best ideas when I'm on the move—either travelling or exercising or just taking a walk." Warren Buffett, CEO of Berkshire Hathaway, states, "I insist on a lot of time being spent, almost every day, to just sit and think. That is very uncommon in American business. I read and think. So, I do more reading and thinking and make fewer impulse decisions than most people in business. I do it because I like this kind of life."[10]

SELF-IMPOSED PRISONS

There are some leaders who severely limit themselves in a self-imposed prison. This locks a person into a very small space, where they will not grow or thrive. Disney and Fuller did not live that way. Sadly, many people never even try to pursue a dream or desire, fearing failure, ridicule, or rejection.

Consider the following story about self-imposed limitations hampering dreams, imagination, and fantasies. Maybe fish don't dream, imagine, and fantasize?

A fish tale

One day, a man went to clean his fish tank. Not having a second tank or bowl, he filled his bathtub and carefully transferred the fish to one end of the tub. Later, when he went to retrieve them, he saw that the fish never strayed from the same spatial area, the size of the rectangular tank.

Fascinated, he watched for a while and even sprinkled fish food on the other side of the tub to entice them to leave the small area. They never did and seemed to be happy to just swim around in that confined space. They created a life of self-imposition, never to know what was on the other end of the tub. The fish were never curious. They were content and comfortable.

Likewise, people exhibit tendencies toward self-imposed captivity. We seem to gravitate to building walls between our dreams and reality. Notice that as we grow older, our imagination becomes more limited. Society places limits on us through social etiquette, rules, and expectations—often imposed by stereotypes. Schools teach us what is and is not, what should and should not be. Job descriptions tell us what we should do every day. Even chronological age tends to focus on limitations rather than possibilities. Eventually, we become comfortable and dependent with sameness. We feel safe in our own little corner of the tub as routines become a way of life, and we sail toward our death in comfort.

The habit of letting your mind go and breaking through the barriers of everyday life's self-imposed limitations is vital for a leader's success. Confining yourself can make anyone become a prisoner of the mind and spirit. Unlimiting yourself requires courage, risks, and belief in yourself to succeed.

Recall a quote by William G. T. Shedd about ships: "A ship in harbor is safe, but that's not what ships are for." Great leaders must be curious and explore; they must follow their dreams.

REACHING FOR THE MOON!

If you are as old as I am, you will no doubt recall President Kennedy's "Moon speech" in 1961. The leader of our country provided a guiding vision created by imagination and fantasy to an entire country and generation. It was truly about the impossible, but his vision and imagination set the tone for our lives for decades to come. If you have not read it in its entirety, I recommend you look it up on your search engine and read the entire transcript. It is a good speech!

> We choose to go to the Moon in this decade and do the other things, not because they are easy, but because they are hard, because that goal will serve to organize and measure the best of our energies and skills, because that challenge is one that we are willing to accept, one we are unwilling to postpone, and one which we intend to win.[11]

Obviously, Kennedy did not stay within the confines of his tank!

Food for thought

Think outside the box. Dream, fantasize, and imagine. Doing so will make you a great leader. When is the last time you let go and dreamed of the impossible? Try being a kid again and let your imagination go. Fantasize. Dream of impossibilities. There are no rules and no one to tell you that you can't.

CHAPTER 2

DON'T PICK UP ALL THE DOG HAIRS

"I don't see any dog hairs!"

—Abbey Dwinnells

An important yet seldom discussed theme in leadership literature is the concept of letting go or simply yielding. Contrast this with the aggressive pursuit to succeed. Leaders are often portrayed as strong and decisive; they always want to win. Western culture sees aggression and ambition as positive traits and letting go or yielding as negative, a sign of weakness. Those who are in leadership positions know it is impossible to win every battle, and it takes a true leader to know when to fold 'em.

SHIKATA GA NAI

Not long after the Pearl Harbor attack on December 7, 1941, many Japanese descendants living in Hawaii and on the West Coast were interned into camps surrounded by barbed wire and armed guards. Commonly accepted among those imprisoned Japanese Americans was the concept of *shikata ga nai*,[1] which translates to "It cannot be helped" or "We have no control over this event." Although the meaning is essentially similar to its Western analogy—"It is what it is"—the perspective is different. For most Westerners, the idea implies hopelessness. There's nothing we can do about it, so all is lost. But to the Japanese, it is the acceptance of reality. Things happen—both bad and good. The event was simply meant to be, and perhaps it will lead to a predestined state. This explains why so many of those interned made the best of bad experiences. They built gardens, held classes for kids, celebrated birthdays and holidays, and enjoyed get-togethers, parties, and conversations. Despite the harshness of the circumstances, everyday life continued. They weren't mired in self-pity and self-defeat; they forged ahead and yielded to forces they were unable to control. Their victory was the ability to live in peace and contentment despite the circumstances. They simply let go and blended into their situation.

This belief suggests that it is okay to fail, because it cannot always be helped. Perhaps something else, maybe something better is in store for us. Yin and yang are about complementary opposites—black and white, dark and light, win or lose—whereas *shikata ga nai* is somewhere in the middle. It's about compromise and acceptance of something that just is—a good quality for a leader to have.

It has taken many years for me to cultivate *shikata ga nai*, but once I had mastered it, it became a very useful tool for high-level meetings, dealing with people and projects, and personal life matters. I once found myself challenged by the art of yielding to my own daughter and her nefarious dog.

Charlie

I encouraged my soon-to-be-sixth-grader daughter Abbey to make all As on every grading period for the entire year. "Do that," I said, "and I'll get you a puppy!"

Since I was the primary household cleaner, I always resisted having animals in my house. But I felt safe about this challenge; Abbey had come close in the past but had never achieved straight As.

To my dismay, she handed me a swift defeat when she presented her final report card. I soon found myself walking out of the breeder's home, clasping a floppy yellow Lab puppy—Charlie.

At first, it was okay to have Charlie in the house. He was small and cute, with disproportionately large paws. He was like having a newborn babe in the house; everyone wanted to cuddle and dote on him. I admit he was well behaved, and at first, I fleetingly thought maybe this wasn't going to be that bad. He stayed with Abbey in her basement bedroom and rarely came up to the main part of the house.

Not long afterward, when I returned from a short business trip, Charlie had doubled in size and roamed all around the upstairs areas. Mounds of dog hair were piled everywhere. Yikes! What to do?

I had to take immediate action before the situation got out of control; after all, I could not have dog hair all over my clean house. I built a large pen, using two-by-four lumber and chicken wire mesh. Soon, Charlie was "evicted" from the house. He could live in his new home forever. "Shed all the hair you want now, Charlie!"

It wasn't long before he tactfully began to bark—only occasionally at first, but it became more incessant and louder with time. Then he started chewing and gnawing. He tore through the wood and wires as easily as if he were consuming ice cream or sipping melted butter. I thought I was dealing with a giant rat! Even the drywall the pen was placed against had huge holes where he had chewed through. I had no choice; he returned to the house, where I thought the situation would improve, but he began gnawing at the kitchen drywall too!

Charlie continued to grow into a behemoth of a dog and began shedding more hair. He slobbered, he drooled, and his tail hurt like a whip. There were billions and billions of dog hairs everywhere—in the carpet, on the furniture, on everyone's clothing—not to mention the mites and dander each hair fiber contained.

Every time he lay on the floor, I'd make him move and then proceed to vacuum that spot. I cleaned like a fiend: in the morning, in the evening, after work, and even before bed, seven days a week, all hours of the day! I might as well have been cleaning in my sleep. I was going crazy trying to pick up every single strand of dog hair, and it wasn't working.

Exhausted, one day, I quit. I just couldn't take it any longer. I was tired of cleaning when nothing stayed cleaned. When I announced my retirement from household chores over dinner one evening, no one said anything; they continued to go about their business of eating. No one cared.

I soon found a new passion for building gardens in my backyard. First, it was a dahlia garden, then a gazebo, followed by a water garden complete with three-tiered waterfalls. I added a pergola and a Japanese garden a year later. It became a haven for me. It was beautiful—and off-limits to Charlie!

I substituted a chance to succeed (my gardening) for failure and misery (yes, that would be Charlie!). Psychologists call this *compensation*. I took up the hobby of gardening and building things to replace my obsession to keep a clean house. I discovered I was good at creating things of beauty. It gave me a sense of fulfillment and contentment. A very good thing happened to me from an adverse situation, because I let go. I yielded to a greater force (Charlie's indomitable follicles and Abbey's love for Charlie). I conceded that I could not win the dog hair battle, so I moved on to bigger and better things.

Some leaders have difficulty evolving this concept, but it is an important one if you are going to succeed. You cannot win every battle, but you can alter your course by conceding. Then take a different path and do something better!

Food for thought

Have the courage to yield. Let go. It may take you to a better place. You cannot always win and, occasionally, must accept less than perfection. Just let it go and build a garden! Think of a time when you yielded something because you knew you could not succeed, but later realized that it worked out for the better.

CHAPTER 3

DON'T TURN DOWN FAME

"Failure is the key to success;
each mistake teaches us something."
—Morihei Ueshiba

After President George W. Bush and I did a town hall presentation in Youngstown, Ohio, on the strength of health care in 2004, there was a lot of local interest from the media. I was front and center on every local television, radio, and newspaper outlet for a while.

My adolescent daughter Sarah asked, "Daddy, are you famous?"

I thought about it for a second and replied, "No, Sarah. If I were famous, you wouldn't have to ask; you would just know. So that makes me unfamous!"

After a pause for effect, I declared, "But I do have FAME!" and grinned widely at her.

She looked puzzled, shrugged, then walked away.

FAME was the acronym I had invented for the leadership classes I taught at local medical and graduate schools. It is formed from the first letters of each of these words: failure, adversity, mistakes, and enemies. I use the acronym to emphasize the important lessons that can be learned from these experiences. Because I embraced them—especially failure—and learned valuable lessons, it has given me great success.

FAILURES ARE VALUABLE EXPERIENCES

Some years ago, while running on a treadmill at a Salt Lake City hotel, I experienced an epiphany. The view from the workout facility was the beautiful Wasatch mountain range. Many trails were visible along the hillside, but none of the trails ever traversed the hill straight on. They went sideways, zigzag, and sometimes even went down before they headed back up. It occurred to me that in order to get to the top of the mountain, sometimes you must go back down a few times (a metaphorical failure). Then I thought about leadership and realized it is much like these trails—and so is life. We make mistakes and often fail, but by learning from them, we can progress. So I came up with the Principles of Failure:

- **Recognize your failure**
- **Embrace and accept it**
- **Learn**
- **Be optimistic**
- **Take action**

Recognize your failure

Sometimes people are oblivious that they even failed. For example, maybe you failed to make your point clearly to someone and they carried out the wrong task. In this case, you may think they failed, but *you* did. It is imperative that we recognize that failure. This is self-awareness, a vital emotional intelligence characteristic.

Embrace and accept it

Own your failure! Embrace it! Don't shy away from it as if it will go away. It belongs to you, so take responsibility and get something positive out of it.

Learn

Failure is an opportunity to improve. Self-reflect and think about moving forward. Write about it in your journal.

Be optimistic

Don't look at it as if it's a negative experience—assume you are going to make something positive out of a negative. What is the good that resulted?

Take action

Do something about it. Don't let failure go to waste. Tell others and teach them about your experiences. Of course, there is nothing more powerful than your own experiences, but it may make people think or even reassess their own failure in a positive light.

When my daughter Emily first started driving and made a left turn into oncoming traffic—resulting in a traffic accident—she was devastated. Scared and feeling like a failure, she swore she would never drive again. But if she didn't learn from a minor accident like this, would she have had a bigger, more consequential mishap later in life? Perhaps this saved her life or someone else's in the future.

THE BEST LEADERS FAIL OFTEN

The best coaches of organized sports teams were rarely the best players of their sport when they were younger, and superstar athletes rarely make great coaches in their later days. Phil Jackson, for example, was the former basketball coach for the Chicago Bulls and the L.A. Lakers. Combined, his teams won 11 NBA championships. In college, he played at a small college in South Dakota and was a power forward for the NBA's New York Knicks but spent much of his time as a reserve. Mike Krzyzewski, another average or above average basketball player in college, became a superstar coach at Duke University, winning five NCAA tournaments and a dozen ACC tournaments.

Bill Russell, the former Boston Celtics basketball player, became a rarity when he became a player-coach in the 1966–1967 season and went on to win two more NBA world championship titles, adding to his nine before retiring in 1969. He was rare in that he became a stellar player and a great coach, leading the Celtics to 11 NBA championship titles in 13 years.[1]

Ted Williams, Larry Bird, Magic Johnson, and Wayne Gretzky were superstars, but their coaching skills in their later years were average at best. Common sense tells us that, perhaps, superstar athletes would make the best coaches. Ironically, their stellar ability is probably why they never do make good coaches; they've rarely failed. They had enormous God-given talent and never had to learn how to do things; they just knew.

This brings back the lesson that, in life, failure always leads to learning. Whether they are superstar athletes or super brilliant doctors, they typically make bad teachers and mentors, because they have never faced much adversity or failure. If they have never had to learn, then they cannot teach and show others how *not* to do things. They cannot give good guidance or coach and teach effectively, because everything always came so easy to them. Many become micromanagers.

Here is one more example of failure and adversity creating greatness.

I have seen the following chronology of a man's disappointments in different ways, but they still tell the same story. This person was born on February 12, 1809, to a poor farmer family in a one-room log cabin. His family was forced out of their home in 1816, and he lost his mother when he was nine years old. He lost his job and was then defeated when he ran for the state legislature in Illinois in 1831. He failed in business in 1833 but was finally elected to the legislature in 1834. But then his fiancée died in 1835, and he had a nervous breakdown in 1836. He was defeated in a run for Speaker of the House in 1838 and was defeated for nomination for Congress in 1843 but was then elected to Congress in 1846. He lost his renomination in 1848 and was rejected for the position of land officer in 1849. He was also defeated in a bid for the Senate in 1854 and was defeated in his nomination for vice president in 1856. He was defeated for Senate once again in 1858. But he was elected president in 1860.[2]

That's a lot of failure and a few successes. Who is this person? Abraham Lincoln, the 16th president of the United States of America.

Food for thought

Acknowledge that failure is part of everyday life and leadership. It is as common as breathing, walking, and sleeping. Don't let failure stop you from persisting. Embrace the Japanese proverb "Fall seven times; stand up eight!"

CHAPTER 4

DON'T NEGLECT YOUR PASSION

"If you can't figure out your purpose, figure out your passion. For your passion will lead you right into your purpose."

—Bishop T. D. Jakes

Where does passion come from? According to the quote from Bishop Jakes, if we want purpose in our lives, we must first find passion. But from where? We cannot manufacture it on demand; rather, it comes from deep within our heart and soul. It is up to us to discover this through relationships, life events, and chance encounters.

Passion is a deeply felt emotion that leads to enthusiasm or desire for something meaningful. It is like a torch lit by inspiration. I was inspired to climb mountains when, as a little boy, I spied Mt. Fuji from atop a playground monkey bar in my childhood home, Japan. It was beautiful and mysterious; I wondered what was on top. Many years later, after climbing my first mountain (Mt. Shasta, in California), I became passionate about the sport and wanted to climb every mountain I saw! The tranquil view from the summit spiritually resonates with me and allows me to clarify my mind, giving me a better understanding of my purpose. I have now climbed 16 large mountains all over the world, including Fuji, and no longer wonder what's at the peak. Passions nurtured by inspiration will lead to the path of our purpose in life. This is essential to success in life and leadership.

As leaders, it is easy to find ways to motivate people, but it is extremely difficult to embolden a person or a group of people to do something for a cause or belief—to inspire. Great military leaders have this ability. Listen to the speech William Wallace gives while riding his horse in front of hundreds of men just before the Scots go into battle with the English in the movie *Braveheart*. Certainly, these leaders are in intense life-and-death situations with all types of emotions flowing through their souls. When emotions are intense, it is easy to inspire and find passion.

MOTIVATION AND INSPIRATION

Motivation can be viewed as getting people to do something by using incentives, such as bonus money, extra time off, awards, and prizes. Motivating someone is to excite them into action, but that excitement is often fleeting.

Inspiration is often triggered by an external event but stems instead from deep inside. Inspiring events will stir your soul. They will push you to accomplish the right things and often have meaning that lasts a lifetime. For example, droves of young men lined up at military recruitment centers immediately after the Pearl Harbor attack—the same thing happened after 9/11. Yes, they were motivated to protect our country, but more than that, they were inspired.

Motivation can sometimes lead to inspiration. When I was in high school, I wanted to earn an athletic letter from my high school. I made the cross-country team and soon scored enough points to get the letter with the CC emblem. This led me to discover that I like running; it made me feel good, and I enjoyed the solitary and quiet time, along with the competitiveness. It helped boost my self-esteem and provided a sense of belonging. My motivation to earn a letter ended up inspiring one of my greatest passions.

Forty-five years later, I still run—not just for those really cool finisher medals but because it makes me feel good. Of course, being told I look 20 years younger (a credit to my running habits) than my actual age never hurts!

"ONLY RICH KIDS AND DOCTORS' KIDS GO TO MEDICAL SCHOOL"

In the fall of 1972, I began my senior year at North Hardin High School in Radcliff, Kentucky. This was a large county school located three miles south of Fort Knox, a US Army base specializing in tank warfare. Otherwise, farmlands made up most of the countryside.

My guidance counselor—the person who was supposed to help me decide what vocation I should undertake after high school—met with me for exactly three minutes that fall. Her recommendation: join the army. It would give me an opportunity to "grow up," to see the world, and to go to college on the GI Bill when I completed my time. "It's the best thing for you," she encouraged. It sounded good, but it would work only if I survived combat. The Vietnam War was still raging, and none of us wanted to put ourselves in harm's way.

I was disappointed with my meeting. Despite my high GPA and rank in the class, the guidance counselor did not recommend that I continue my education by going directly to college. I spied a couple of college brochures, picked them up, and walked out without a second thought. One brochure was about the medical school at the University of Kentucky. I liked the photos of young doctors in white lab coats with stethoscopes hanging around their necks. One graphic showed three medical students and a professor standing around a skeleton model studying the hand bones. They looked cool and even a bit macho, and I thought, *That's it; I'll be a doctor!*

Excited by this revelation, I couldn't wait to reveal my future vocation plans to my parents. When I told my mom, she stared at me for a moment, slowly shook her head from side to side, and replied, "Only rich kids and doctors' kids go to medical school. You're neither, so you won't get accepted."

What was she talking about? I was immediately upset and reacted like any adolescent whose seemingly good idea has been shot down. I replied in a loud voice, "Watch me, Mom!" and stormed away.

I was disappointed but motivated by my mom's negative comment. I did well in college, majored in biology, and got accepted to medical school. When I got the acceptance letter, I called my parents from a pay phone; it cost me a dime back then. She didn't believe me after I told her about the good news, so I drove home to show her the acceptance letter. They were thrilled and just could not believe their son was going to be a doctor. I had triumphed. I could now relax and enjoy life in my 20s. The hard part was over, I thought.

Dead wrong! I absolutely abhorred med school. It was one of the toughest things I ever did. The first two years consisted of 8:00 a.m. to 5:00 p.m. daily lectures, and exams were given on Saturdays so they would have more time to lecture during the week. I kept thinking about my 20s—the supposed best years of my life—going down the drain, having to give away those precious years to sit in classrooms all day, every day. I started wearing cutoff shorts and T-shirts to lectures and walked around in flip-flops. I let my hair grow and wore granny glasses. I looked like the Asian version of Jesus Christ. Looking back, I was subconsciously protesting being tied down and spending every minute of those four years studying. It was crazy!

The motivation to prove my mom wrong did not evolve into inspiration, passion, or purpose. People should want to be doctors to save lives, to help the sick get better and the healthy to stay healthy. That is why I didn't like med school. I did it for the wrong reasons; the motivation was flawed, and the inspiration was never there.

I learned later that passion can and does evolve. After I had been a doctor for some time, I grew to enjoy the profession. It gave me a great deal of satisfaction, but I was still not impassioned by it. I soon founded a clinic and became the executive administrator, overseeing a large community health center. That proved to be more interesting, but I still lacked passion. Then, one day, a horrific event occurred that became the inspiration for my passion.

THE DAY I BECAME THE SAME AGE AS MY DAD

On Thursday, October 18, 2012, at around 2:00 in the afternoon, I became the same age as my father when he died. He took his own life when he was 57 years, 6 months, and 1 day old. Mom found him in the basement not long after he committed this act. The body was still warm, and his face was moist from tears and sweat. Were these clues of sadness and fear?

Four days later, at the service, as the military chaplain extolled the virtues of life and advised us to never fear death, I studied my dad's face as he lay in the casket, etching his features in my mind so I would never forget. I began to wonder how I would look, feel, and think when I became his age, calculating just when that day would occur.

Twenty-eight years hurriedly passed by, leaving a bountiful trail of events, experiences, and emotions. There were happiness and grief; tears and laughter; marriage and children; cars and a beautiful home; a busy career; pets; graduations; vacations; Christmas, Easter, and Fourth of July celebrations; the *Challenger* explosion, 9/11, and the Gulf War. Many memories anchored my mind in a full and blessed life, but nothing slowed the approaching date and the accompanying anxiety.

As October 18 neared, I could not avoid thinking about my dad and wondered if I had become anything like him. I was consumed with questions about his death—always void of answers. How will I feel at that exact moment of the suicide? Certainly, the same fate would not await me . . . or would it? What were his final thoughts? Did he think about me, my brothers, and his wife while he was dying? Was he sad knowing he would never see us again? Were there regrets once he began the process? Did he get halfway and maybe decide he didn't want to do this any longer? Or did death come instantly, with no time to reflect?

My dad was a good man. Portrayals of him were consistent and abundant: "Would never turn his back on anyone," "wouldn't hurt a fly," and "not a mean bone in his body" were common accolades to describe him. At age 39, he was diagnosed with adult-onset diabetes mellitus, commonly known as type 2 diabetes. This was especially detrimental to a man who found intense passion in cooking and eating.

When the military doctor informed him of the diagnosis in 1966, I think his world started to crumble. About the same time, he received orders to be deployed to Vietnam. The two events prompted him to retire after 22 years of military service. The combination of inactivity and the disease began to take a toll, and he fell into a depression. The disease was insidious, and none of us recognized its symptoms.

His new job as a night postal supervisor required odd shift hours—often in the middle of the night; he never got a full night's sleep. He began to eat whatever he wanted and no longer took insulin as prescribed. His blood sugar levels kept rising out of control. As I look back, it should have been clear that the diabetes led to his depression and that the depression prevented him from properly taking care of his illness. His physical and mental health burdens worked in tandem to destroy him bit by bit.

His family doctor nagged about maintaining better weight control, but the physician failed to recognize or address the ever-growing despondency and hopelessness that consumed my dad.

One day, I found my father crying. He suddenly exclaimed, "If I had any guts, I'd kill myself!"

This angered and frightened me. How does anyone respond to that? I walked away. Much later, I realized he was reaching out—asking for help. Perhaps I had become his last chance to survive. A month later, on a cold January afternoon, he hanged himself in the basement of our home.

Jump ahead 28 years later. October 18 had finally arrived. The weather had been dreary and rainy for several days. Nevertheless, I went outside to sit by my koi pond to contemplate and reflect. While lost in reflection, I noticed how brilliant the autumn leaves had suddenly become. They were glowing oranges, bright yellows, and fiery reds. I looked over my shoulder and saw the sun rising and breaking through the clouds. The warmth and brilliance bathed my face, causing me to squint. Its rays splayed across the dawning sky at just the right angles, displaying magenta, red, pink, and purple.

Suddenly, a warm sense of peace and comfort blanketed me, dissolving the apprehension I had all these years about this date. My dad was "talking" to me. A deep sense of compassion surged through me, and I immediately knew what my purpose was: to help people afflicted with depression and suicidal tendencies. With my position as a CEO and physician, I had the opportunity and ability to affect thousands of people and save many lives through awareness and intervention. I suddenly knew that, after all those years of sadness and turmoil, I would be okay. The day I had wondered about and even dreaded for the past 28 years was going to be perfect.

My dad will remain 57 years, 6 months, and 1 day old, but after this day, I will continue to grow. And I will carry the gift of passion and purpose.

Food for thought

All leaders should have passion. Raw talent, skills, intellect, and desire can go a long way toward success, but you cannot attain your best unless you own passion. It must come from deep within. No amount of money or accolades can make this happen; only inspiration, passion, and purpose will make you a great leader.

CHAPTER 5

DON'T FLY WITH TURKEYS

"If you want to soar like an eagle in life,
you can't be flocking with the turkeys."
—**Warren Buffett**

Tennis was popular when I was in college, during the 1970s. Jimmy Connors, Chrissy Evert, Bjorn Borg, Billie Jean King, John McEnroe, and Arthur Ashe dominated the sport for years. They were all great players, in part because of the exceptionally high levels of their rivals. They possessed amazing, sometimes superhuman moves on the tennis court. Most were unrehearsed, unexpected, and unpracticed, stemming from extraordinary competition.

People I knew loved watching and playing the game and sought to become better players; some joined tennis clubs. For poor college students like me, membership fees to play and learn from coaches at high-end tennis clubs were too expensive, so I would pick up games with those who had no partners. If I couldn't find anyone, I'd practice for hours, volleying the ball against a wall.

Initially, most of the competition I found through pickup games was not very good; that's probably why they didn't have regular partners. I would always win, making me feel like a pro. I began to think that I might be exceptional and even had thoughts of becoming the next Jimmy Connors or the Swedish wonder boy, Bjorn. This, of course, was a false sense of confidence, and my dream quickly disappeared after a resounding beating by a more experienced player who happened to be a last-minute stand-in.

Moping around with my head hung low for a few days after that ego buster contest prompted my no-nonsense, direct-talking, and streetwise friend Garland Scott, a medical student at the time, to give me a harsh verbal lashing about how I'm "the world's lousiest tennis player ever" because I only played with losers or by myself.

"You know what they call a guy who plays against losers and then wins every game?" he interrogated. "Turkeys. That's right, man. Turkeys. You're a turkey loser, Dwinnells!"

He continued the rant and told me that if I wanted to always be a turkey, then keep playing with other turkeys.

"But if you want to fly high and be good at anything and everything, like an eagle, then you need to get into some fights with eagles."

"Something else," he continued to bellow. "Bouncing a ball against a wall by yourself is the worst! Do you think you'll ever let yourself lose, playing by yourself? Hell, no! We call that a double turkey—DT! You can't become great by yourself!"

He stared at me for a few seconds—it felt like long minutes to me—and finally shook his head slowly and said, "Man, you don't want to be a turkey loser or a DT all your life. Go find some eagles!"

His response to my sulky behavior was a wake-up call, like being slapped into reality. This simple advice stuck, and from then on, I gave up my ego and made sure I always surrounded myself with people who were smarter and stronger and had better attitudes than me. When I went to medical school, I made friends with the top students, and later, when I became a leader and a boss, I made sure to hire the best people I could find. I made sure to hang out with eagles and not turkeys. This way, I knew I would always continue to improve and could eventually become one of the best. Turkeys flock; eagles soar!

DON'T GO SOLO EITHER

The second part of Garland Scott's advice was to not go it alone. How do I become better when the only gauge is myself?

David Rockefeller, in his 2002 book *Memoirs*, wrote, "I am always open to and aware of the potential of a new relationship." Although this man was fabulously wealthy and could accomplish anything on his own, he understood the power of relationships and knew not to attempt things alone. In a 2017 obituary, he was described as a shy, insecure, and often lonely child who overcame his quietness to become a leader in banking, philanthropy, and international relations. He became much more powerful and influential through relationships than if he had gone it alone.

Although my Japanese mom's culture supported groupthink mentality, she always taught me to be as independent as I can be. "Never depend on anyone," she always warned. So I grew up wanting to do things myself. When I became older, I felt more "manly" that way—more independent. I was like Jeremiah Johnson: I could do it all on my own. I didn't need anyone else. When I attained leadership roles, though, I recognized the importance of relationships. I did not know everything and could not accomplish all I wanted alone.

I recognized this valuable lesson when I was a resident physician at a children's hospital: A very arrogant attending physician, who never sought advice or second opinions because he called himself a "walking encyclopedia," assumed care of a teenage girl recently diagnosed with toxic shock syndrome. This was a relatively new and deadly phenomenon then, and he had no experience managing the problem. He refused to listen to anyone's advice, especially the one about transferring her to a facility whose physician had more experience in these matters. After a brave struggle, the girl passed. This man was a practicing solo turkey, and a young girl suffered for it.

Leadership is not a solo act. To be effective, we need to work with others, especially those who are better and smarter than we are. That becomes the pivotal point of great leadership: Accept the perspective that others may and probably do know more than you. Learn from them.

A good example is the fictional detective Columbo from the eponymous 1970s television series. On the surface, he seemed a goofy, absentminded detective, always needing help from the criminal to remember things or to clarify something obvious. In part, he wanted to throw them off guard, but just about every time, the criminal would explain things, usually out of tedious frustration, and Columbo would learn something new.

An important part of leadership is to learn from others so we can become better at leadership. Being humble is crucial! Never be so arrogant that you believe you are the brightest and the best.

Food for thought

You cannot succeed without the help of others. Good leaders always build relationships and seek help and advice. When you do, always be sure to surround yourself with people smarter than you.

CHAPTER 6

DON'T BEND PRINCIPLES

"If you start bending principles, they won't be principles anymore."

—**Lucas McCain,** *The Rifleman*

Joni was a bad nursing student—not wicked or immoral, just a very poor academic performer. She was frequently tardy for classes, habitually dozed off in classrooms, had disjointed clinical assessments, and was inconsistent with her medication follow-through. Some of her patients' vital medications were missed. Somehow, however, she managed to survive up to now, her senior year.

As her final academic year neared its end, Joni found herself in a bind. She had already failed one class and now faced one more final exam in a class where she had a failing grade. Joni knew she needed a minimum score of 73 percent to pass the course but also knew she was totally unprepared, since she had skipped many of the lectures and had not read any of the books or handouts. If she failed this class, Joni would be drummed out of nursing school; the College of Nursing had a strict "two strikes and you're out" policy.

Joni scored a 69 percent, even after her instructor tried to help by adding a few extra bonus points. She pleaded her case to her teachers without avail. Joni failed the program; there was no way around it.

Wait! Not so fast. Enter Joni's mom!

Learning of her daughter's expulsion, Joni's mom got involved. She immediately resorted to an aggressive and demanding attack against the professors that included name-calling and colorfully explicit and threatening language. Her message was that the instructors had no idea what they were doing. Joni was a victim of their incompetence.

Despite the insults and threats, the professors stood their ground: "Joni failed the test, fair and square. She failed the nursing curriculum and is not qualified to be part of the nursing profession," declared the professors. "We cannot and should not violate policy, tradition, and rules. She will not graduate with such a poor academic and clinical performance."

Frustrated and angry, Joni's mom demanded to see the dean.

Flash ahead to graduation day. To everyone's amazement, Joni appeared at the graduation ceremonies. All robed up in graduation regalia, she confidently marched across the sacred stage of high achievement and accomplishment to receive the coveted bachelor of science degree in nursing. Her classmates, professors, and anyone who knew her sat silently stunned, with jaws agape, as they witnessed the dean proudly smiling, shaking her hand firmly, and giving her a diploma. Joni's mom, wearing a nicely placed corsage near her right jacket lapel, busily took photo after photo of her smiling and happy daughter. Her family was so delighted.

What's wrong with this picture? Joni was a poor student but somehow managed to get by. When she objectively could not pass a class and did not meet all the criteria for graduation, a person with administrative authority allowed her to graduate by overriding all objective information and the professors' decisions. Did the dean buckle under the mother's pressure? Yes, he did. But why? How did the nursing faculty feel when their authority was commandeered by the dean? How did Joni's classmates feel when she was able to "earn" a degree just like them without meeting all the requirements? What kind of nurse would she become? Could she end up hurting future patients because she was never a good student?

Sadly, but probably rightly so, Joni failed to pass her state nursing board exams and now works as a secretary at a used-car dealership. The dean was reassigned to another part of the university, but his reputation followed, and he was always seen as a leader who could not be trusted. No one respected him.

Joni's mom was disappointed by her daughter's performance, and so she made an effort to force the state nursing board to pass her daughter through her local state congressman's office. This time, it did not work. Joni's former nursing faculty continued to adhere to their principles, and the department became one of the most successful for their nursing board exam pass rates by their graduates.

WHAT EXACTLY ARE PRINCIPLES?

Principles are an accepted or professed rule of action or conduct. They are a fundamental, primary, or general law or truth from which others are derived. Different circumstances and disciplines have their own esoteric sets of principles. For example, in nature, the sun always rises from the east and sets in the west. Without water, most living things would not survive. We cannot sow seeds in September and expect a crop by October. In economics, it's about supply and demand: If the supply is low and the demand is great, then the price is high. In my medical profession, there is the Frank–Starling law, a principle describing the blood-flow dynamics of the heart as it relates to the heart muscle cell stretch and contractility. For example, the volume of blood flow out of the left ventricle increases with the stretch of the heart muscle cell that causes a more forceful contraction.

There are many types of principles—moral, nature, accounting, management. I had a textbook in med school titled *Harrison's Principles of Medicine*. It described the right way to practice medicine. Most leadership principles have some core commonality, such as honesty, integrity, trustworthiness, loyalty, fairness, empathy, respect, and accountability.[1] Without these, no one will respect you enough to follow you. The concepts and characteristics do not differ much from some of the basic elements of emotional intelligence: self-awareness, self-regulation, empathy, motivation, and social skills.

In Joni's case, principles were clearly bent, and emotional intelligence was not used by the dean. He was afterward considered "shady" because he overruled the faculty's recommendation that this student fail. By doing this, the nursing faculty learned that his integrity, loyalty, and trustworthiness were not up to par with their standards. Will the professors ever trust the dean—their leader—again? No way! Will they lower their standards because it doesn't seem to matter to the university anyway? I hope not, but maybe some will. The consequences of unprincipled leadership can be profound.

Bending principles can have disastrous effects for leaders in many ways, but particularly when it comes to trust. How do people trust you after you've betrayed them? Just one incident can have a permanent effect on your reputation. Leaders must be very careful they never bend principles! Their leadership will never fully recover.

Food for thought

As leaders and in order to gain respect, you must follow a set of principles and never bend them. Lucas McCain is correct: Once you start bending principles, they won't be principles any longer. A good leader must practice good principles. Do the right things for the right reasons, and do them the right way. Good principles keep things in order and help a leader realize their mission and accomplish their goals consistently. Have you ever bent principles?

CHAPTER 7

DON'T PASS THE BUCK

"I never trust an executive who tends to pass the buck. Nor would I want to deal with him as a customer or a supplier."

—James Cash Penney, American businessman

A recent story from the *New York Post* with the headline "Pinch 'Hit'ters!"[1] caught my interest. A murder contract had been put out by Tan Youhu, a real estate developer. He wanted a rival developer, who had previously sued Mr. Youhu's company over a building dispute, killed. Xi Guangan, a hit man, was hired to commit the murder. But Xi, in turn, hired another hit man, Mo Tianxiang, paying him half of what he (Xi) got. Mo then paid another guy, Yang Kangsheng, who then hired yet another hit man, Yang Guangsheng. A few months later, the second Yang hired Ling Xiansi. Each hit man was offered a lesser amount than his predecessor.

Ling (the last assassin for hire on this list) didn't do the killing but, instead, informed his target, the real estate developer, that there was a plot to kill him. The developer, seeing a cash opportunity for himself, schemed with Ling to fake his death so they could split the money for his supposed assassination.

All five hit men were eventually caught, each casting blame for the failure to kill the developer on their hires; however, they all got prison sentences—along with Tan. The intended victim survived unscathed and even made some money from the plot to kill him! Obviously, this is an exaggerated—if not humorous—example of passing the buck.

PASSING THE BUCK

The idiom *pass the buck* has an interesting history since its inception in the early 1900s. It is known to have originated in poker games, typically seen in saloons and riverboats of the Old West. During card games, an object—usually, a knife with an antler handle—was placed in front of the person whose turn it was to deal the cards. The knife came to be known as a buck, since only male deer have antlers. So, when it was time for a new dealer, the buck was passed to the next player in line. If a player did not want to deal, he would place the buck in front of the player next to him, literally passing the buck.

The act of passing the buck can be portrayed to mean either relegating the responsibility for something to another, as in the "Pinch 'Hit'ters" story or, more commonly, to shift blame to someone else to avoid responsibility for a perceived failure.

President Harry S. Truman famously popularized the phrase *the buck stops here*. He even had a sign on his desk with those words on it. His intended meaning was that he would take responsibility for decisions and that no excuses should be made by anyone else nor should blame be put on anyone else.[2]

People pass the buck every day. Usually, it is used as a form of cover-up: "I didn't know that it happened, but my chief of staff did, and he should have informed me! I'll make sure I get to the bottom of this scandal and that people will pay!"

PASSING THE BUCK ILLUSTRATED

Someone didn't do their job. One way to decipher the "Pinch 'Hit'ters" story is to view it from the perspective of people passing their responsibilities on to others to accomplish a specific task. In this case, the job to kill the developer went from one hit man to another until the last one ratted on his predecessors. When a project, job, or assignment is passed on to others repeatedly, the proper end goal is often not met. Exact communication may have been lost, or the details may have become blurred as the assignment kept being translated by the next duty shirker. The urgency of a matter often does not resonate or is not properly conveyed to those carrying out the assignments.

The lesson in this story is that sometimes you cannot pass the buck if you want something done correctly and in a timely manner. Strong oversight may be needed, or perhaps the job needs to be done by the person who conceived it. This is where a solid system of management, leadership, and communication becomes important to assure things are being completed the way you want them to be done.

SHIFTING THE BLAME

Interestingly, some people will pass the buck ahead of anticipated trouble, as happened to me in second grade. Some fellow students and I were on a recess break, and one of the boys, Kerry, found a pile of smoldering ashes in the corner of the playground. Excitedly, he called us over to investigate.

One of the three boys who showed up said, "Hey, why don't we try to get a fire going from these ashes!"

So, we stripped small pieces of paper and dry leaves to get them to catch fire. Soon, a small spark caught, and in no time, we had a steady flame going. The bell rang after a few minutes, bringing our experiment to a halt. We stomped out the flames, and as we walked back into the classroom, we noticed Cindy Lou, a classmate, whispering into our teacher's ear and staring at us while we made our way to our desks.

Mrs. Fletcher looked mad. After the second bell rang to start back with classes, she walked to the front of the room and said with a mighty, stern voice, "Which of you boys were playing with fire during recess?"

My three friends and co-conspirators took furtive glances at one another but didn't say anything. Suddenly, Kerry, the kid who found the smoldering ashes in the first place and who had definitely partaken in our fire party, raised his hand and said, "Mrs. Fletcher, I saw those boys playing with the fire," and he pointed his fingers at each of us. He continued, "I told them not to do that, but they just wouldn't listen to me!"

Certainly, this is tattling, but it is also shifting blame—passing the buck—to avoid getting caught and diverting the attention and responsibility to others.

We got in trouble, and poor Kerry never did have any friends after that. Kerry didn't want to be punished, but he had no problems turning on his friends to get *them* punished.

People in positions of power or in very public ranks, such as corporate leaders and politicians, often shift blame because their failures are likely to be noticed by others and can cause repercussions, such as a loss of status, rank, or even employment.[3]

In a study published in *PLOS ONE*,[4] researchers found that most people *expect* corporate leaders and politicians to shift blame, even though people don't believe it is an appropriate action and don't really like those who do pass the blame on to others. Does this mean politicians and high-visibility leaders get a free pass? Sometimes. Kerry passed the buck, and he got a free pass, because the rest of us followed a "boys' creed" to never tattle on their friends. However, Kerry spent the rest of his boyhood alone. Although, he did grow up to be a local politician.

In my experience it is always a good idea to recognize your mistakes or wrongdoing and to fess up to it. Be proactive, and own it, then publicly apologize. We often see leaders hesitate to apologize, believing it is a sign of weakness; however, in a study published in the *Journal of Business Ethics*,[5] researchers found that leaders who apologize can positively influence future perceptions of leaders—themselves and others. Furthermore, apologizing runs counter to the popular belief that blaming others reflects a sorry act of leadership and has beneficial effects in the long run.

The bottom line is don't pass the buck. Own it!

Food for thought

Good leaders take responsibility for the good things that happen, as well as the bad. They don't blame others and do not shift blame for failures and mistakes. By accepting responsibility, the leader will be viewed with respect and will be seen to have high integrity. Don't pass the buck to others. Deal with your mistakes. Own your failures. And learn from them. When's the last time you passed the buck?

CHAPTER 8

DON'T BE A SHOEMAKER

"If you don't have time to do it right, when will you have the time to do it over?"

—John Wooden

My father-in-law, a well-respected and internationally recognized authority in engineering science, was also one of the most down-to-earth men I have ever known. Born and raised in Romania, he and his parents escaped the rapidly approaching Russian Communists toward the closing days of World War II. He spent 47 days in the bowels of an oil tanker crossing the Atlantic to Ellis Island, New York. At the age of 14, not long after arriving, my father-in-law entered first grade due to his English language deficiency, but he attained his PhD from Carnegie Mellon University just a few years later. He became a professional civil engineer and a university professor for 46 years and authored numerous technical papers and seven college textbooks still used at universities worldwide.

He had a quirk of using a mixture of "old country" colloquialism and blue-collar vernacular to describe certain people or events. The term *shoemaker* was a name he gave to people who were not very good at tasks but tried to pull themselves off as experts. "Nothing but a shoemaker," he would declare when something was not done properly. As an engineer, he would get upset if the work did not meet exact specifications.

Some leaders get caught up in the "I know and can do anything and everything" attitude. The good leaders will know when they are in over their heads and need to bring in experts. This self-awareness is vital to successful outcomes. Leaders should always surround themselves with the best support, but there are times when we also need fresh eyes on a problem or project—perhaps better experts. After all, we don't want to be shoemakers.

My dad always told me, "You have to know and work with people to help you succeed." Since the primary purpose of a leader is to provide vision and direction, leaders need to cultivate and nourish relationships to do things right.

A DIRTY RAT STORY

When we moved to the United States in 1961, my parents were poor. My dad, a hulking 6'2" 200-plus-pound soldier, was a sergeant (E-7) in the US Army and didn't make much money. To help with the family income, Mom sewed military insignias on uniforms for soldiers who could not sew or didn't have others to help.

We settled into a small two-bedroom clapboard house located on Walnut Street in Vine Grove, Kentucky. Owned by an elderly gentleman by the name of Mr. Cook, the house came to be known as the Cook House. This also happened to be the home of a nondescript rat—a medium-sized gray long-tailed rat. Dad thought there was only one, but later, I read that rats were social and hardly ever lived by themselves. There had to be others around.

My dad said that we were too poor to buy a trap, so he was going to sit guard after nightfall in the kitchen where he could easily spot the varmint. Then, at the right moment, he was going to whack it with the broom with all his might. He carefully laid out some American cheese for bait and assumed a forward-leaning stance in the dusky room. Through clenched teeth, with a cigar protruding out the left side of his mouth, he said, "They only come out in the dark because they're nocturnal. That is the only time you can get 'em."

Peeking through the small crack of the kitchen door with a child's intense curiosity, I could make out his silhouette, broom cocked, smoke spewing from the cigar, ready to pounce on the creature that had invaded our tiny abode.

Told to keep quiet in case our movements or voices would scare the rat away, Mom and I sat on a bed in the adjoining room, laughing silently and joking about my dad's seriousness. Occasionally, we heard loud smacks as the broom fibers struck hard against the linoleum flooring, making us chuckle more. The rat eluded his fate for three straight nights.

"He's quick—really quick! Smaller than I thought—almost like a mouse," Dad declared and reluctantly admitted that this tiny creature might be smarter than he was. More determined than ever, he built a trap out of a King Edward cigar box. He sat it on its side, with the lid propped up by a skinny stick tied to a string. He filled it with morsels of rat goodies and proceeded to assume his position in the middle of the dark kitchen. With the other end of the string grasped deftly between his fingers, he patiently waited for the rodent, now nicknamed Wilson after the villainous gunslinger in the 1950s movie *Shane*, to show his rat face!

Suddenly, hearing noises in the kitchen as if two grown men were in a fight, Mom and I rushed into the kitchen. We found Dad lying on the floor with the closed cigar box under his chest, panting and proudly saying, "I got 'im! Got 'im! I got the dirty rat!"

He quickly jumped up with the box in hand and rushed to the bathroom, filled the tub with water, and threw the rat in. I didn't know why he wanted to toss the rat into the water. Was he that dirty? A splotch of dirt on his gray coat was visible as he immediately began gliding smoothly on the water surface—gracefully, as if water surfing. He even took a few dives and swam underwater as if he were playing his own version of Marco Polo! I think he was having fun. We watched for several minutes, mesmerized, unable to take our eyes off him.

Dad, now perplexed, suddenly bent over and grabbed the rat by its long tail, then ran to the back door, twirled the rat around twice over his head, and launched it into the field. We could see some rustling of weeds and concluded that the rat had lived to see another day.

My dad had spent several days hunting this rodent, using cheese, crackers, and peanut butter for bait and spending hours in the dark. He filled a bathtub full of water—how many gallons of perfectly good water went to waste? The rat did not die, and I'm sure he came back the next day if not that night—probably even with friends and family—to scour our house for more food.

Dad should have done it right in the first place: called an exterminator or splurged for an $0.89 trap and rid the lot of them once and for all! As it turned out, the rat came back, and the numbers multiplied over the next few months. We never did discover the true population of these rodents living with us in the Cook House, but we knew Dad didn't get rid of them.

Do it right the first time! If you are not good at a task or do not understand the problem, get a professional to help you do it right. You will usually know at the beginning of any project whether you will succeed or not. Consultants, experts, and professionals cost more, but it will be a huge savings of resources and time. Shoemakers can cost a lot in the long run.

Food for thought

Leaders are never experts on everything. They need help just like everyone else to get things done well and to do them right. Don't skimp on help and expertise. In the long run, leaders will save resources and be ahead in their goals by getting expert help and not by being shoemakers. Have you ever tried to do something yourself because you didn't want to pay for an expert to do it . . . then later discovered that it ended up costing more than if you had paid for an expert to do it in the first place?

CHAPTER 9

DON'T BE A SQUIRREL

"Be decisive. Right or wrong, decide. The road of life is paved with flat squirrels who couldn't make a decision."

—**Unknown**

Have you ever wondered what goes on in a squirrel's mind when it spies a grove of oak trees full of acorns and the only obstacle that lies in the squirrel's path is a road with lots of traffic? Imagine this scenario taking place in a squirrel's mind:

The Wishy-Washy Squirrel

Lots of nuts over there!
Gonna get 'em!
Yup, sure am.
Making my move. Now!
No, wait . . . truck!
Okay, now!
Nah, better not.
Should I, shouldn't I?
Should I, shouldn't I?
Okay, halfway . . .
Nope, bad timing. A car!
Okay, coast is clear!
Go . . . now!
Uh-oh!

Don't be a squirrel! Sometimes, quick decisions based on present information, analysis, and intuition are required in leadership. Once you make the decision, stick with it. This squirrel was unable to succeed because of its indecisiveness and failure to use any intellect or gut feeling. It paid the price.

It is crucial that leaders make solid decisions; this applies to everyday living as well. Not only do these decisions sometimes have to be quickly made, but they must be firmly held as well. Two tools needed to accomplish this are analytics and your gut.

A few years ago, I was faced with a horrific dilemma. As the health-care power of attorney holder for my mom, who was afflicted with Alzheimer's dementia, I was forced to make a decision to either treat her recently discovered liver cancer; letting medical science subject her to the harsh side effects of chemo, radiation, and surgical treatments; or let it be. The treatments would possibly extend her life a few more months, but the fear and the suffering from side effects would have lowered her quality of life.

As a physician, I fully understood the technical, analytical, and scientific logic behind doing everything medically possible to help my mom. But I also knew that the best decisions should never be made with just data and analytical statistics.

In medical school and residency, we were trained to make assessments and plans of a patient's medical problem based on *both* subjective (feelings and perceptions and not always using solid facts) and objective (facts, based on test results and exam findings) information. We called them SOAP notes: S for *subjective* information the patient would tell us about their condition—how they feel, where it hurts. O stood for *objective* information and data we obtained through examining the patient and obtaining lab tests or X-ray examinations. The A was *assessment*—conclusions derived from putting the S and the O together. Finally, the P was the *plan*, the decisions made based on our S, O, and A. It is an excellent process to analyze problems and make decisions.

First, know that accurate and reliable information is paramount; false information leads to poor and inappropriate decisions. Next, explore feelings. "I've been feeling sick for a long time. I've got chills and am puking sometimes" are subjective, whereas objective information—"These red bumps all over my body have been there for three days now"—is often observable and testable. In this example, things like vital signs, blood work, and X-rays are considered objective findings too.

The analysis and conclusion of feelings and findings (assessment) will lead to well-informed decision-making. Having a rash all over the body, blood work findings, and negative chest X-rays (O) could suggest a viral syndrome. My decision (P) would be to treat this symptomatically.

My mom did not remember much of her daily life. She did happily remember her younger days, spending many days musing and laughing about a happier and carefree time. I wanted her to spend her last days in peace, not in fear of all the needles and medicines that would make her weak and sick if I chose the *do something* route dictated by my analytical thinking. I also didn't want her to be frightened of the strangers in white coats who talked incessantly about things that provided anxiety and didn't make any sense to her. And I didn't want her to spend hours in the cold and sterile environment of medical clinics, hospitals, and doctors' offices. So I made the difficult gut decision to do nothing and to let her die in peace.[1]

This was the result of analytics (I understood medical science and knew the statistical outcomes) and gut (I didn't want my mom to suffer, and my gut told me to let her go) combined. As we all know, there isn't always a right answer; sometimes, you just need to follow your gut.

MAKING DECISIONS

When the analytical process just does not work or is strongly contrary to my instinct, I find myself becoming the indecisive squirrel. It has always worked out better if I ultimately go with my intuition.

To apply my decision process, I like to think in terms of a scale. Think of a line graph, where the far-left side represents *do nothing* and the far-right end is *going for the optimum, best thing that can happen.* Continuing with the previous example, I have concluded this patient has a viral syndrome. I can choose to do nothing (the patient will get better through their own natural defense mechanism), or I can tell them to take Tylenol or Advil for fever or pain control every four to six hours for two to three days, drink lots of fluids, and rest. I can also decide to act anywhere along that spectrum; maybe I want the patient to only take Tylenol as needed and to continue normal activities. This scale tool works well and helps keep you grounded when you're making decisions for a variety of situations and projects.

Most decisions involving emotional projects initially come from the gut. You may leave out that SOAP process. For example, a feel-good project like starting a medical clinic for the homeless will prompt you to make a quick decision to support it. Later, however, the analytics portion kicks in. How much will it cost? How many homeless people will I serve? How long will it take to start the program? Who will help me plan this?

Consequently, feel-bad issues have a similar process: Causing a child to get the wrong vaccine will result in an immediate termination of employment for the staff nurse who made the mistake. However, again, the analytics kicks in. Did anyone get hurt? How many times has this nurse made this mistake? What is the financial and quality cost of this mistake? Was anyone else involved? Were labels correctly applied to the vaccines?

Emotional projects and issues usually have a pattern of gut + analytics. Longer-term projects and issues tend to have a more analytical approach. Here's another example: Let's say I want to build a new office building. Do I really need a new building? What is the cost? Where will I get the money? How big do I build it? There are so many decisions in life and leadership. The hardest decisions are the ones that deal with emotions, especially as it relates to family matters.

Let's get back to the squirrel, now more confident:

The Confident Squirrel

Lots of tasty nuts over there!
Gonna get 'em!
After those two cars, I'll go!
Look both ways!
Okay, all clear!
Making my move.
Now . . . go!
Phew! Made it!
Yum!

Food for thought

Making decisions is an important quality for leaders and may involve a variety of strategies. Most decision-making processes use a combination of analytical and tangible informational sources. However, our best decisions typically emanate from the gut, especially when the situation has no clear solution or answer. Never neglect your gut feelings!

Take a moment to watch a squirrel in the park or in the woods. They seem to be unfocused and random. Do you ever get this way?

CHAPTER 10

DON'T FAIL TO PRIORITIZE

"Things which matter most must never be
at the mercy of things which matter least."

—Johann Wolfgang von Goethe

I was once asked in an interview what my daily work consists of as a CEO. I didn't have to think too long: I conduct and attend lots of meetings; advise, problem-solve, make decisions; create and follow through with new projects. Doesn't sound like much, but this makes up about 30 hours of an 8-hour workday! Prioritizing is an essential skill that leaders need to master.

In my leadership classes, I frequently perform a demonstration with rocks, sand, water, and a jar to explain why we must prioritize our lives: I have a large jar—like the kind that contains pretzel sticks; a large dill pickle jar works too. I ask my students how many large rocks (about the size of baseballs and softballs) will fit into this vessel. Some yell out seven; others say eight or even nine. Let's say six fills the jar up to the lip. I will then ask the class if this looks full. They always yell out a resounding yes.

I then pour smaller rocks, the size of pebbles, filling the spaces between the large rocks. Amazed, now only about 70 percent of the students say it is full, while the rest skeptically say no.

Now I pour sand. This fills the other voids between the smaller rocks. I ask again, and now the answer is about 50 percent saying it is full and about 50 percent saying it is not completely full yet. Finally, I pour the water.[1]

The point of this exercise is that if we fill our days with small rocks, sand, and water, a metaphor for the little things we deal with all day long such as emails, telephone calls, text messages, petty gossip, and nonsensical items, we will never be able to put our most important things—the big rocks—in first.

Food for thought

Leaders especially need to prioritize what is important. Make sure you put in the big rocks first; otherwise, you will never get them in later. Think about a typical day in your life. Do you get pulled in many different directions and at the end of the day you didn't accomplish what you intended?

CHAPTER 11

DON'T BE FOOLED

"Fool me once, shame on you.
Fool me twice, shame on me."

—**Proverb**

In 1961, when my parents and I traveled from Japan to our new home in the United States, we had a layover in Anchorage, Alaska. Dad gave my mom money to purchase snacks at an airport shop. Being unfamiliar with the currency in America, she returned from the snack shop and gave my dad the change—not knowing whether it was correct or not. He took one look and stormed over to the salesclerk, yelling about the wrong change. Later, he told Mom that "the people who work in these stores try to cheat foreign travelers every chance they get because of their money confusion." Mom always kept her guard up after that—probably with a little paranoia spurred by this incident. She warned me at an early age that there are people who may want to try to fool me, especially if I ever get into positions of power. "Don't believe everything people tell you," she advised.

Everyone has been fooled at some time or another. After arriving in San Francisco from the Anchorage stop, we took a cross-country trek to Louisville, Kentucky, by bus. We stopped at numerous bus stations, and on one of the legs, an unkempt man sat next to me. I feared him at first, but he began doing tricks with a nickel, making it disappear. Then, suddenly, he'd "find" it behind my ear. How did he do it? Was he just fooling me like the airport salesclerk fooled my mom?

As leaders, we must be especially careful not to be led astray by these cons. When leaders are surrounded by many issues and when numerous decisions need to be made, it is far easier to seek quick and targeted solutions from others. But beware! I've learned that there are a lot of "foolers" around—people who profess to be experts. Many appear bright, and for a moment, we believe them, but it eventually becomes clear that they are not the experts we thought they were. They are characterized by taking shortcuts, cheating, and almost always wanting to take the path of least resistance. Many act overconfident because they are trying to overcome their shortcomings by being a know-it-all. They often possess low self-esteem and frequently boast.

Over many years of encountering different types of foolers, I have been able to categorize some of these.

KNOW-IT-ALLS

How can any one person possess so much knowledge about so many different topics? These people never say, "I'm not sure" or "I don't know." They can discuss any topic as long as you are listening. They are often opinionated and judgmental, and worse yet, if we don't do what they recommend (since they are such experts), they will let us know that we'll regret not taking their advice. We've all met this type, but don't be fooled. Use them sparingly and always take what they say with a grain of salt.

DONE-IT-ALLS

How about those who have done everything imaginable and unimaginable? This category is a kind of cousin to the "I know everything" person.

An emergency room doctor I once knew—a nice enough fellow—bragged about all the things he had done in his lifetime of 36 years. At various stages in his life, he was an NFL football player (Denver Broncos), an Olympian—twice in two different sports (swimming and downhill skiing), an executive who drove fancy sports cars with beautiful women at his side. He was even a reigning equestrian champion, specializing in dressage events. All this, and he still found time to go to med school and become an emergency room doctor.

As if this was not sensational enough, one late evening when it was slow in the emergency room, he related his experiences while serving in Vietnam. In hushed tones—I'm not certain the reason for the surreptitious nature of his voice—he boasted that he was a combat soldier during the Vietnam War and became a genuine hero. As a 19-year-old private, he single-handedly defended a mound of land near the demilitarized zone. According to this "warrior," the event was kept secret from the public due to its covert nature. The "brass" told him that he would probably receive the Medal of Honor for his bravery once they declassified the event. Hmm . . . didn't I see a movie like this?

Watch out for these folks too! You will know these are con stories when you see the sensationalism.

SMOOTH TALKERS

In a recent article, Harvey Weinstein was described as someone who had the gift of gab. He could "talk a hungry dog off a meat bone," according to acquaintances. This type of con can get you to do things you don't want to do. Don't make quick decisions when these folks try to get you to do something, especially if they want you to do it quickly. If it doesn't make sense and it doesn't feel right, put it on the back burner and ponder it. Be careful!

One subcategory of smooth talkers is those who never disagree and always praise everything. "You're right, Dr. D," they say. "I agree with you!" These folks may be ego strokers for you, but it becomes quite boring after a while. For me, they are "empty heads," as my mom would call them. They have nothing worthwhile to contribute, so please don't waste your time with them. Remember, as a leader, you want to surround yourself with people who are not afraid to be contrary with your ideas or values. A car does not move forward without friction.

PARAPHRASERS

How about those who paraphrase everything you say as if they are the ones who came up with the idea or knowledge? They do this because they have no ideas of their own and must use yours to make themselves think they are important to you. These people are not dangerous; they are just annoying and take up your time and occupy space in your mind. Try to avoid them.

THOSE FOCUSED ON APPEARANCES

Appearances are not everything. I've worked with people who look outstanding. They are well groomed and look like royalty. But many are clueless when it comes to thought processes. I hired a chief operations officer who came to us very highly recommended. He looked and acted like a chief executive officer, but it was soon clear he had very few gray cells in between those ears. Once, I was angry with him for making a very bad decision and told him that he's like a nutshell without the meat. He slapped his bald head—straight from a *Three Stooges* episode. He didn't understand the nutshell reference but got the fact that he made a mistake.

It is not hard to pick these people out. Just don't let their façade fool you. The meat is more important than the nutshell.

LIARS

Those who start their sentences with "I'm going to tell you the truth," or "I'm not lying," or "I'll be honest with you" should raise a cautionary blip on your radar. Certainly, these phrases may be innocent and used for emphasis; however, for me, it raises suspicion. Perhaps it may be a function of my personal life experiences with adversity or perhaps the position or status I hold, but I have difficulty trusting people who use these phrases.

ONE-UPPERS

We have all had conversations with people who do not listen or care about anything you say. They never ask questions because they are not interested in what you have to say. They are simply egotists who thrive on boasting their adventures and accomplishments to an audience—you! You are just a prop who provides cues to center their talking points. It is curious and often incredulous that they can always one-up you on just about anything. Their events, topics, and ideas are always better, bigger, stronger, and have happier endings than yours.

NEGATIVE NELLIES

Watch out for the Negative Nellies. The glass is always half empty, and the world will end tomorrow for these people. They are constantly warning you about every negative thing that could happen. If you listen, some of the information is sensationally eye-popping, but don't believe a word unless you have witnessed it firsthand. This is where we get the saying "There are always two sides to a story, and somewhere in the middle is the truth." As a leader, make sure not to get sucked into the negative world vortex. You will have difficulty getting out.

PEOPLE WHO DISTORT THE TRUTH

This one is prevalent, as we see elected officials and media frequently try to lead us astray by telling one falsehood after another. They cannot seem to stop. This is not exclusive to just politicians or the news outlets. Everyday people engage in this practice too. I recently had a case where two employees were fired for stealing time and tossing important patient medical information into the trash. They went to the National Labor Relations Board (NLRB) and made up a story about how they were trying to organize a committee to help improve working conditions but got shut down by our administration. The NLRB took the case, and I spent thousands of dollars that could have been used to improve access and quality of health-care delivery but instead had to use it to defend my organization against lies.

These are just some of the classic small talkers and small-minded people who are full of nonsense and never get anywhere in life. Leaders just need to know these people exist and to not waste too much of their precious time with them.

You don't want to be fooled! You cannot afford to be led astray through bad advice. If you are leery about folks with these characteristics, don't become an empty head and follow their advice. Be aware that they exist, and do your best to avoid them.

Food for thought

Use your intuition when listening to others for advice or information. Be aware of and vigilant for people who will lead you astray. If something—an idea, a thought, or a way of doing something—does not feel right, then it probably isn't. Your gut will always be right. Be alert for ulterior motives. Do you know anyone in your life who fits any of these characteristics?

CHAPTER 12

DON'T TURN A GRUDGE INTO REVENGE

"Weak people revenge. Strong people forgive. Intelligent people ignore."

—Albert Einstein

A nursing professor once stole my two-year research on childhood obesity, later publishing the work under her name. I was rightfully upset with her. How could she take credit for my work? I learned that day not to share important unpublished research data with just anyone.

Not long after this incident, a brand-new medical director filed a whistleblower protection status for herself before alleging that I oversaw fraudulent Medicaid billing practices, inappropriately expending federal grant dollars and confiscating employee pension funds. Following a yearlong investigation by the FBI and the state attorney general's office, costing both taxpayers and my organization hundreds of thousands of dollars, the case was dismissed for a complete lack of evidence. It turns out that the medical director had recently earned a master's degree in public health, giving herself the impression that she was more qualified to be CEO than me. She wanted to oust me and take my job. I was never upset, never held a grudge, and never contemplated revenge, because I knew her allegations were nonsense. I was more upset with the FBI and the attorney general's offices for not being diligent by requiring more evidentiary information from the accuser before beginning an investigation. Both cases were a waste of resources, and I was grateful that I never let my negative emotions consume me.

Life and leadership events often create situations where enemies are expected. Jealousy, disagreements, perceived wrongs, or threats often lead to the emotion of anger that may give rise to grudges and acts of revenge. Leaders are especially susceptible to a daily barrage of true and false information, accusations, ridiculous gossip, and endless personnel situations that can lead to professional discontent and can ultimately arouse anger, providing an opportunity for revenge or for holding a grudge.

GRUDGES

Someone carrying a grudge might not act or show any physical signs, but they're being consumed from the inside out. Don't let it eat you alive. As leaders, we face all types of people and difficult situations every single day that may cause ill feelings or that may be insulting to us. Most are petty. If we don't let it go and clear them from our minds and emotions, grudges will eventually influence us to make bad decisions or to act in ways that make us look less executive and more like petty losers. People will shy away and soon lose respect for our leadership.

There are plenty of stories of how people have forgiven a wrong that resulted in the lifting of a heavy burden. They felt a release and were able to go on with their often successful lives, simply because they relieved themselves of a grudge.

An incredible story about letting go is the one about Louis Zamperini, the World War II US Army captain and former Olympic long-distance runner who was held as a prisoner of war by the Japanese.[1] For over two years, Captain Zamperini was tortured and mistreated mercilessly, living in depravity. Despite these horrid conditions, he survived and came home. Suffering from a horrific bout of PTSD, Zamperini "found God" at a Billy Graham evangelistic crusade—a turning point in his life, where he learned to forgive. Soon, a trip to postwar Japan to confront his torturers and inform them of his forgiveness for their atrocities helped dissipate his grudges, leading to a productive and happy life until his death at 96 years old. He led a respectable life and was rewarded many times throughout his life.

As a leader, we don't want to fill our minds with negativity. The mind has a finite capacity. Why fill it up with hatred or vengeful plots? Fill it up with good things! Use your brain to create, imagine, and solve the unsolvable. We always have a choice, and choosing the right one will make us better leaders.

REVENGE

Revenge takes grudges one step further—to action. It can become very dangerous!

Growing up as a "half-breed" kid in post–World War II Japan was no beach party. Many Japanese resented the American soldiers who now occupied their land and who had killed or maimed their loved ones during the war. Not having typical Asian features, I was often glared at by native adults while the kids yelled obscenities, threw rocks, or whacked me with sticks. When this first happened, I ran to my mom.

Her response: "If they call you names, just hit them. If they throw things at you, hit them again. You have to pay them back so they don't do this to you anymore." I quickly learned to return their attacks—sometimes more aggressively.

When my army dad had orders to report to Fort Knox (Kentucky), we moved to a small community near the military base called Vine Grove. The local kids were lifelong residents and came from a long line of Smiths, Joneses, and Thomases—families who dominated the area and had settled there many generations ago. I wasn't one of them, so I didn't fit in. I didn't look like them, and my last name was very different. It didn't help that I couldn't speak the language. Just about every day, I would hear other kids say, "Hey, Jap. What cha' doin', Jap? Huh, Jap? Gonna beat the crap out of a Jap today!"

Mom kept telling me that no one should ever say anything bad about other people, so that's why you have to pay them back. So I did, although the American kids were a bit tougher than the Japanese ones because they were bigger. As I got older, she told me, "Don't worry. Someday, they'll get paid back!" I assume she was referring to Karma.

My parents were good people, but they grew up during difficult times. Dad lived through the economic depression of the 1930s and had sometimes gone days without food, proper clothing, and even hot baths. Mom lived through the horrors of US warplanes dropping incendiary bombs on her hometown in Japan, watching people burn alive or being maimed so horribly that no one could tell who they were.

Like Maslow's hierarchy of needs for food, water, warmth, rest, and shelter, people who live through difficulties and suffer from a wide variety of emotional stress develop defense mechanisms to protect their basic needs of dignity, pride, and fairness. Hatred, distrust, and revenge became defense tools. They were used to protecting themselves, equalizing their misfortunes, and reducing the risk of continually being victims. They didn't know or understand how else to solve problems or deal with situations.

As I grew up and became a physician and CEO, I found myself in many leadership roles. I have often witnessed people who didn't like something or didn't agree with someone say they were going to pay that person back. Or when I worked hard for something and was successful, jealousy would emerge, and people would try to make me look bad as if I didn't deserve the accolades that went with it. They wanted what I had, and they were going to attack me to get it. I learned that seeking revenge is a real waste of my intellectual resource and a big waste of time.

I had a chief operations officer who worked for me for many years. She was tough and wasn't popular or well liked by many. So they would try to "get back at her." This always backfired and resulted in either termination or resignation of the "avengers." They were so consumed with hatred and anger that they let their guard down, putting all their energies into how they could achieve their revenge. Besides completely wasting their time and energy, these people ultimately lost their jobs, because they couldn't focus and do their own work.

Revenge has consequences, and it may come back to bite you. The following is the true story of an attorney general in Pennsylvania who let revenge run her life and career.

On October 24, 2016, the former attorney general for the Commonwealth of Pennsylvania, Kathleen Kane, was sentenced to 10–23 months in jail for illegally disclosing details from a grand jury investigation to embarrass a rival, then lying about it under oath. Kane secretly leaked documents from sealed files to embarrass and harm former state prosecutors she believed had made her "look bad." She was convicted in August 2016 of one felony count of perjury, obstruction of justice, and seven misdemeanor charges. Kane resigned the next day.[2]

Judge Wendy Demchick-Alloy said Kane took the attitude of "off with your head." "This case is about ego—the ego of a politician consumed with her image from Day One," the judge said. "This case is about retaliation and revenge against perceived enemies who this defendant felt had embarrassed her in the press."

The prosecutors called her crimes "egregious" and pushed for jail time. They said a paranoid Kane ruined morale in the 800-person office and the wider law enforcement community through a calculated scheme to embarrass rival prosecutors who had left the office.

Ms. Kane had been riding high. She had the political world within her grasp, becoming a rising star in the Democratic Party who was making a name for herself. She was smart, tough, and ambitious, but vengeance got the best of her. Instead of focusing on the good and letting go of negativity, she was determined to get back at her rivals for what she perceived was a wrong before that strategy eventually backfired and caused her professional demise. What a sad shame for Ms. Kane.

I think Mom was partially correct: People who do wrong will get paid back someday, and the wrongs will be righted. Karma will happen.

OVERCOMING THE URGE FOR REVENGE

The best strategy to ward off the urge to hold on to grudges and seek revenge is to address the situation as quickly as possible and avoid escalation. Once you become aware of an "enemy," confront the situation through dialogue, reckoning, and reasoning.

Colonel Paul Tibbets, the man responsible for organizing and carrying out the mission to drop the first atomic bomb over Hiroshima, was marred by competitor pilots who wanted to fly the airplane holding the world's first nuclear weapon. The plotters were working behind the scenes to sabotage Tibbets's preparation efforts in an attempt to make him look weak and incapable. When he discovered the plots, instead of playing petty games and seeking revenge, he immediately went to the commanding officer, and together they quashed the adversaries. Soon after, Colonel Tibbets flew his B-29 Superfortress (the *Enola Gay*, named after his mother) into history.[3]

Another strategy is to simply forgive and just let go. How many stories are there of horrific crime victims who forgave their offenders and were able to go on with their lives like Louis Zamperini? Many share similar experiences and describe forgiveness as "relieving heavy burdens on their hearts and souls," "a new lease on life," or "uplifting." It is not worth the toxicity that grudges produce.

Food for thought

To paraphrase Norman Vincent Peale, resentment and grudges don't harm the person you are angry at. But every day and every night of your life, they are eating at you.

Think of a time when you were so upset about something or someone that you tried to get revenge on them. How did it work out for you?

CHAPTER 13

DON'T DRESS LIKE A WARTHOG

"If you look good, you feel good, and if you feel good, you do good."

—Georges St.-Pierre

When my daughter Abbey and I completed our climbing expedition up Mt. Kilimanjaro in the summer of 2018, we were excited about the upcoming safari adventure on the Serengeti plains. It is such a lively region, teeming with animals of every species imaginable. One peculiar animal we frequently observed was the *ngiri* (warthog). However, many natives, as explained by our Tanzanian guide, Ahgri, referred to them as *pumbaa,* meaning "foolish" or "dumb," because of their erratic and impulsive behavior. As many may recall, Pumbaa is also the name of the warthog character in Disney's *The Lion King* animated movie. They are hideous-looking creatures with a miniature body and an oversized head adorned with large tusks. Ahgri informed us they are dirty animals and that no one likes them because they snort and are so ugly. He added, "They even like taking baths in the mud. Warthogs do not dress well!"[1]

People often formulate opinions from first impressions. According to scientists, a person starts to form impressions of a person after seeing their face for less than one-tenth of a second.[2] Immediately, we decide whether the person is attractive, trustworthy, competent, extroverted, or dominant. There are stereotypes that humans associate with certain physical characteristics, and these stereotypes can greatly affect a first impression. For example, politicians who are more attractive and put together are often considered more competent. The debate between John F. Kennedy and Richard M. Nixon broadcast on live television depicted Mr. Kennedy as a suave, well-dressed, confident, calm, and collective candidate, while Mr. Nixon was sweating and appeared dark and even rogue. Kennedy won that election over the better-known Nixon.

When I was going through the certification process to become a certified physician executive, a requirement was to attend a weeklong seminar that included a variety of topics on how to be an executive. One was the notion—or probably better said, the art—of dressing up like an executive. I thought it was a bit nonsensical—just window dressing in my mind. I could not take it too seriously. I did find it amusing that the lecturer even brought a few models along, who displayed the proper attire for the executive look. Before that lecture, I believed in the concept of what makes *you* who *you* are is "inside" *you*—the heart, mind, passion, kindness, and so on. This is what determines and measures your attributes, not how you look on the "outside."

As the years hurtled by, my idealistic views began to diminish, and I adapted to some more realistic cultural norms. I recognized that appearance may actually be a very important aspect of a leader. We are like a walking billboard, advertising our essence through our exterior appearance. For example, General George S. Patton was an impeccably dressed military officer who exuded a tough, warrior-like image. His uniform was perfectly tailored, adorned with colorful campaign and heroism ribbons. He even sported a .45 long Colt single-action revolver pistol at his side.[3] This look gave him a presence of toughness and commanded respect. He led by intimidation; that was his trademark.

There are many other examples of how appearance defines the persona and character of an individual. In the television series *Columbo*, Lieutenant Columbo, a brilliant detective played by Peter Falk, sported a slovenly and disheveled look, portraying absentmindedness and a not-all-there personality. His trademark and ever-present wrinkled raincoat and cigar completed his character. With this presentation, no one took Columbo seriously, especially the bad guys, so they relaxed, mistaking him for a fool. Ironically, that's how he always got his man: They let their guard down.

Bruce Wayne and his ward, Dick Grayson, were depicted as playboy rich guys, dressed to the hilt, but when they changed into their Batman and Robin costumes, they became tough crime fighters. The same goes for Superman, the Green Hornet, and Spider-Man. The clothes created a façade, and they became someone else while people saw them as superheroes.

Your appearance has a lot to do with the way people act and how others formulate opinions about you. It is a normal process for us to profile just about everyone and everything based on physical appearance. If you want people to respect you as a leader, the image you create can be as important as the underlying traits that contributed to your leadership status. First impressions will dictate much of the way people react to you.

WHY IS IT IMPORTANT TO LOOK LIKE AN EXECUTIVE INSTEAD OF A WARTHOG?

When I was in my 20s and had just completed medical school, I wanted to be profiled as just a "regular" guy. Growing up as a half-Japanese, half-American kid in both countries, I never fit into either society or culture because of prejudices. First impressions by members of both countries determined that I be treated in a manner different from how the typical citizen was. As a young adult, I didn't want people to treat me differently just because I was now a medical doctor. I even had the notion that anyone could succeed in medical school. What made me so special that I had to act differently and be treated differently? I purposely dressed in blue jeans and T-shirts, along with my favorite sandals, as I took care of my patients. Of course, I got a few odd glances by a few patients, but most thought I was cool. At least, that is what I thought of myself.

As I got more involved with the business of medicine, I found myself meeting with important leaders such as hospital administrators and local business executives—those with power and influence to help my clinical program succeed. Very few took me seriously at first because of their perception of me as a physician with no business sense. But I soon realized my clothing was probably inappropriate. I looked like a homeless guy carrying around a stethoscope.

With time, I realized that the façade was important. I recognized that if I looked important, then people would take me and my ideas more seriously. It was amazing what a necktie, sport coat, and a pair of high-end loafers could do for my image. I dropped the jeans and the sandals and later earned an MBA degree and added that to my business card. Now armed with another degree and the impeccable dress of my alter ego, I gained even more credibility and respect. Maybe I do know something about the business of medicine. I started to get heard at meetings, and my opinions were taken seriously. I was asked to be on community, state, and even national boards of directors. Even the president of the United States came to visit me, and we hosted a town hall meeting together.[4] This gave me leverage and persuasive power to do the things I thought were right and believed in regarding health-care delivery programs. I was never a conventional man, so it took a while to recognize the importance of convention and façade when it came to power and the ability to move things along. Therefore, I learned to clean up and look good.

Social scientists have myriad findings that support dressing up.[5]

The following concepts were taken and paraphrased from an article titled "10 Unexpected Ways Your Clothes Can Change Your Mood." I added a few more important items when it comes to appearance.

Your clothing can make you feel powerful

The power tie is a real thing, according to a study published in *Social Psychological and Personality Science.* Researchers had certain people wear formal business attire and complete a series of five experiments that challenged their cognitive processing abilities. Those who dressed up felt significantly more powerful and in control of the situation than their underdressed peers.

Your clothing can make you feel more confident

Whenever I wear nice clothes, I feel more confident about myself. It makes me feel as if I am wearing some form of shield that will protect me from self-conscious negative features about me.

Your clothing can make you a better thinker

In addition to feeling more powerful, the same study also showed that the subjects who dressed in business formal clothing could think faster on their feet and had more creative ideas. The scientists speculated that how you dress can change your perception of the objects, people, and events around you—sparking fresh ideas and a new point of view.

Your clothing can improve your posture

I walk and sit with a straighter posture when I wear nice clothes. No one sits in meetings with a suit and tie while their leg is hanging over the arm of a chair.

Your clothing can make you exercise harder but make it feel easier

Athletes in red clothing won more events in the 2004 Olympic games than their competitors in blue, which inspired researchers to wonder whether that was just a coincidence or whether there is something special about the color red. The study, published in the *Journal of Sport and Exercise Psychology*, showed that people who exercised in red could lift heavier weights and had higher average heart rates, indicating they were working harder than those wearing blue, even though both groups reported similar rates of exertion.

Your clothing can make you smarter

According to a study published in the *Journal of Experimental Social Psychology*, dressing in clothing that is associated with intelligence, like a doctor's coat or a pilot's uniform, may not only make you look smarter but may actually make you act smarter too. Researchers gave doctor's lab coats to subjects (none of whom were doctors) and then asked them to perform a series of complex tasks. Those in white coats made significantly fewer mistakes than the people in street clothes. The scientists then repeated the experiment, but this time gave lab coats to all the participants. However, they told half the people they were doctor's coats while the other half were told they were paint smocks. Again, the people in the "doctor's coats" performed better on the tests, which shows that it's not just what you wear but also what you *think* of what you wear that matters.

Your clothing can help you get your way

This one is for those who hate haggling over a car price or negotiating a house contract. According to research published in the *Journal of Experimental Psychology*, your clothing can give you an edge in an argument. Subjects were divided into three groups: They dressed in either a suit, a pair of sweats, or their own clothing. They were then put in a scenario where they had to negotiate. The people who were dressed better routinely trumped those who were dressed down. Even more interesting, the men in sweats showed lower testosterone levels, which further reduced their aggression.

Your clothing can make you more honest

There may be a sneaky side effect of wearing knockoffs, according to a Harvard study published in *Psychological Science*. Researchers gave people fancy new sunglasses, telling half of a group they were designer, while the other half was told they were counterfeit. Those wearing the knockoffs were more likely to cheat during a subsequent game and expressed more suspicion of other players. Wearing fake clothing, it turns out, may make you feel like a fake—and may make you assume others are also being fake.

Your clothing can make you want to work out

Wearing running shorts and sneakers first thing in the morning is more than a comfy way to run errands; seeing yourself in athletic duds could motivate you to hit the gym on your way home from the store. "It's all about the symbolic meaning that you associate with a particular item of clothing," said Hajo Adam, PhD, a Northwestern University researcher and author of the famous lab coat study.[6] "I think it would make sense that when you wear athletic clothing, you become more active and more likely to go to the gym and work out."

Your clothing can cheer you up

Researchers from the University of Queensland interviewed people and observed their clothing. Often, people dress how they would like to feel or how they would like others to think they are feeling. In other words, people put on a happy sweater along with a happy smile, even if they are feeling down. And it works, especially if we wear clothing that has gotten us compliments in the past or that brings back good memories.

Your clothing can make you lose weight

Wearing a snug-fitting pair of pants, tightening your belt a notch, or even tying a ribbon around your waist underneath your clothing can give you a subconscious signal to stop eating as soon as you are full. "A number of French women wear a ribbon around their waist and underneath their clothes when they go out for dinner," explains fitness guru Valerie Orsoni.[7] "It keeps them conscious of the tummy—particularly if the ribbon starts to feel tighter as the evening goes on!"

Dress even affects children

Dress and appearance have such a positive effect on people at the business and social level, but what about children? This appears true for school-aged children when evaluating the relationship between school uniforms and school and behavior. Studies reveal that kids who are required to wear uniforms at school do better. Virginia Draa, assistant professor at Youngstown State University, reviewed attendance, graduation, and proficiency pass rates at 64 public high schools in Ohio. Her final analysis surprised her: "I really went into this thinking uniforms don't make a difference, but I came away seeing that they do. At least at these schools, they do. I was absolutely floored."

Draa concluded in her study that those schools with uniform policies improved in attendance, graduation, and suspension rates. She was unable to connect uniforms with academic improvement because of complicating factors such as changing instructional methods and curriculum.[8]

WHAT DOES IT TAKE TO LOOK LIKE AN EXECUTIVE?

During my time as a practitioner of being the CEO doctor in blue jeans and T-shirts, I hired an older gentleman who became my COO. He was always impeccably dressed, had good posture, and had great manners. Whenever he and I would go to meetings, people who didn't know me thought he was the CEO. They treated him with great respect and often gave me questioning glances, as if saying, "What's he doing here?" Ah, the power of looks!

There are several additional things that can be done to make yourself appear more like an executive. I've learned these tips after years of ditching the T-shirts.

First and most important is that you have the knowledge, experience, and capabilities to be the executive you are. This requires many years of education and experience and cannot be gained simply by looking good. Confidence through experience contributes to an aura of the executive look.

If you meet with people on a higher level or want them to take you seriously about a certain matter, make sure to wear a nice suit dress or professional attire for women and a coat and tie for men.

Good grooming is critical. Keep your hair combed and get regular cuts; trim your nose and ear hairs as well. Smell clean. Brush your teeth often and get regular dental checkups and cleaning. Good teeth and no bad breath are part of the image an executive portrays.

Have good manners. "Sir" and "ma'am" are great to use anytime. Open doors for others. Ladies are always first.

Smile and have an affable countenance. Be approachable.

Stay in good shape and health.

Maintain a good posture.

Keep your office tidy, comfortable, and executive-looking.

Spruce up your business cards. Make it impressive. I received a cool business card made of wood from someone who works for the Davey Tree Expert Company. I keep it because I like the feel of it and the novelty. Make sure you put your credentials on it too.

I once did an experiment where I made two sets of business cards. One had all my credentials (MD, MBA, CPE, FAAP), and the other had just my name. Whenever I gave my plain card, I was treated in the same manner as anyone else, but when I presented the card with all my stuff on it, I was treated like royalty. Very peculiar how people are!

How you write your emails, texts, and letters also makes a difference in how you are perceived. When I receive emails without a salutation or a complimentary close, I don't take it very seriously and think less of the person. The same is true for texts that have lots of errors. I've seen resumes from prospective employees with misspellings or mistaken use of capitals, and these prospects did not get an interview.

All these tips offer credibility, respect, and integrity. So dress as if you are the king, and don't look like a warthog.

Food for thought

If you are the boss, make sure you always portray yourself properly and professionally. Impressions play an important role in people's perception and respect of your character and integrity. Have you ever gone to a nice restaurant dressed sloppily? You were probably kicked out. But, if you are dressed nicely, you are often treated like royalty!

CHAPTER 14

DON'T BE A JAMOKE

"The difference between stupidity and genius is that genius has its limits."

—Albert Einstein

My father-in-law, a walking dictionary for slang words, often referred to men who were slovenly, lazy, and not the brightest crayon in the box as *jamokes*. Some people self-deprecate themselves as jamokes when they make dumb mistakes. Tom and Ray Magliozzi, for example, on National Public Radio's *Car Talk*, often referred to themselves as a couple of jamokes.

For a long time, I thought this was a made-up word. Imagine my surprise when my wife found it used in a fictional book about a bank robbery gone awry. This motivated me to look it up, and yes, there it was—a real word!

Appearing at the end of the 19th century, *jamoke* referred to coffee—a blended word of *java* and *mocha*. By the 1920s, it became slang for someone who lacked mental abilities beyond those of a cup of coffee.[1] The word isn't used much today, but it can still be used to describe an ordinary, unimpressive, or inept person—typically as a term of mild or joking disparagement for a man.[2]

ABSTRACT THINKING

Besides talent, knowledge, desire, hard work, and a great deal of emotional intelligence, a good leader must have strong cognitive abilities to solve problems, plan, and think abstractly.

Most of us have made stupid mistakes. We are jamokes at one time or another. Just because we may be in leadership positions does not make us immune to them or prevent us from doing foolish things. Much of the ability to think through problems has to do with the development of abstract thinking.

Abstract thinking centers on ideas, symbols, and the intangible, while concrete thinking focuses on what can be perceived through the five senses: smell, sight, sound, taste, and touch.[3] Fascinated with Neanderthals, I once heard in a lecture that the reason they became extinct was because of their lack of abstract thinking capabilities. The lecturer gave a scenario that depicted the Neanderthal living on one side of a river that happened to have fewer animals and food sources than the other side. Across the river was a lush and verdant forest, harboring many animals and much edible vegetation. The Neanderthal was described as not being able to think abstractly enough to foresee that if he moved to the other side of the river, his life would improve drastically. Instead, he stayed where he was, living a life of want and need. Were they jamokes? Perhaps, but having the ability to think about ideas and to problem-solve will certainly help us all find the other bank.

Jean Piaget, a developmental psychologist, believed that children develop abstract reasoning skills during the formal operational stage—around 11–16 years of age—which is defined as the last stage of development.[4] It appears there are different degrees of development and that most people use a combination of concrete and abstract thinking to function in daily life. Some people tend to favor one mode over the other.

Interestingly, a professor in one of my undergraduate psychology classes lectured that 80 percent of the world's population never attains abstract thinking capabilities.[5] I have never found resources to support this claim, except for my written notes in that course. Subjectively, however, I do believe there are quite a number of people who I encounter on a daily basis who do not attain the abstraction abilities to solve problems and develop critical thinking. Perhaps I am one of them.

OF MICE AND A MAN

We had just bought our dream home and had spent way beyond our means for it. A two-story, completely bricked home in an exclusive neighborhood—I thought I was the cat's meow! I had made it.

After being in my castle for about a month, I spied a small furry creature waddling nimbly next to the concrete basement walls. I was flabbergasted and could not believe that my new home was also home to a mouse. Not being a killer of animals or insects, I bought a live trap and stocked its interior with a couple of peanut-butter-laden Ritz crackers.

The next morning, excited like a kid waking up on Christmas morning, I hurried down to the basement to see if I had caught the gray rodent in my trap. Sure enough, I heard scraping from the inside of the aluminum metal trap and could see movement through the small air holes lining the top. I was surprised when I peered into the trap. There were two mice! Aha! So the mouse had a friend! I took the box with the two amigos to the woods about 50 feet behind my house and let them go. They scurried away as if they were two cute little boys going to the fishing hole for the day. My battle with the mouse—now mice—was over. Mission accomplished as I rid my home of these pests.

I kept the trap out just in case there was another friend around. I was surprised when lo and behold the next morning I had trapped three more! The following day, there was another one, then another the day after. Two more, then three after that. I couldn't believe that my precious home was so infested!

One day, a light bulb went off in my head. Were these the same mice that, perhaps, kept coming back for more? The last set of three were still in my trap, so I cleverly (at least that's what I thought of myself at the time) painted a stripe of typewriter correction fluid on their gray backs, then set them loose about another 50 feet farther into the woods. The next morning, there they were: three striped mice in my trap!

It took me a while to put my thinking cap on, but after I did and my abstract thinking kicked in, I recognized the possibility that I did not have a mice infestation but an illusory perception based on boomeranging mice. They were the same rodents returning over and over to a free meal followed by a pleasant walk in the woods. I felt like a real jamoke when I realized my blunder.

It is important for leaders of any organization to constantly think of all possibilities of vision, problem-solving, and ideas. An excellent way to think abstractly is to always ask questions—what, why, when, where, and why not. (*Why do I have so many mice in my new home?*) Always take the answers and analyze them to come up with and understand a conclusion. (*Maybe they are the same mice coming back after I released them.*) Finally, develop solutions. (*If I paint the mice, I can see if they're the same ones when I capture them again. If so, I will release them somewhere far away from my house.*)

If leaders keep this simple and basic paradigm in mind, most of us will keep our jamoke habits at bay. This is what will create great leaders. Regardless, even exemplary leaders have their jamoke moments!

Food for thought

Leaders need to constantly problem-solve through clear thinking abilities and constantly asking questions of what, why, when, where, and why not. Be a clear and levelheaded thinker and not a jamoke. Have you ever been a jamoke?

CHAPTER 15

DON'T MAKE FRIENDS

"Good friends care for each other,
close friends understand each other, but
true friends stay forever, beyond words,
beyond distance, and beyond time."

—Anonymous

Friendship and love create a bond so important that disruptions of this bond can be devastating. Think about people who die from a broken heart after the loss of a loved one. Because they are so overwhelmingly grief-stricken, they can no longer go on, occasionally leading to death from stress-induced cardiovascular diseases and even suicides as a result of severe depression.[1]

Such is the story of Anne Hewlett Fuller and her husband, Richard Buckminster Fuller. Her obituary, appearing in the July 4, 1983, edition of *The New York Times*,[2] describes a 65-year marriage between Anne and the famous inventor of the geodesic dome. Astonishingly, he preceded her death by 36 hours when he suffered a fatal heart attack while visiting his wife in the hospital. She had been hospitalized because of complications from a stomach operation and was in a coma when he visited. It is reported that Richard had always promised his wife he would "go first."[3]

The profound power of friendship and love is so great and so essential for life that difficulties forming or maintaining friendships can result in neuropsychiatric disorders like autism and depression. Forming bonds is an essential part of humankind, because it helps promote successes and improves health and even survival.[4] Although the story of Richard Buckminster Fuller and his wife may be an example beyond friendship, it serves as an example of how powerful it is to become emotionally involved with others.

As misleading as the chapter title is, I do not advocate having no friends; rather, I warn you to be careful while forging new friendships in a work environment, especially when you are the boss. The boss's responsibility is to assure the success of the company and business through following rules, maintaining organizational structure, and keeping the mission always in mind. When there are friends involved at the workplace, this can become a bit dicey.

It is human nature for most people to jockey for a good position with the top brass. But when friends are mixed in, they may get special privileges or be allowed to bend the rules to make their lives more pleasant. They may even get better pay, might receive higher status, and may not get in trouble when they really should.

To be able to understand why it is important for leaders to refrain from making friends at the workplace, we need to be aware of the emotional aspects of relationships. It is difficult to be both a leader and a friend to people who report to you because of the challenges of emotions. The primary reason is that emotional conflict can lead to a decision-making dilemma. Some of these decisions, especially those dealing with raises, promotions, reprimands, and terminations, will be influenced by relationships such as friendship and family. Most places of business have strict rules on nepotism and romantic relationships at the workplace. Interestingly, however, you never see rules against friendships. How do you tell people they cannot make friends?

THE ANATOMY OF FRIENDSHIP

Friends are made through shared emotions, shared experiences, and common likes and dislikes. Scientifically explained, friends engage in affiliative interactions, such as spending time together, conversing, vocalizing, grooming, huddling, sharing food, and forming alliances against others.[5] Likes, dislikes, laughter, joking, teasing, and conversations can create a sense of bonding and togetherness. It is fun and natural to have friends, and it creates a sense of belonging and even well-being. But know that bonding can sometimes create emotional conflicts.

There are two aspects of friendliness at the workplace. First, know that most subordinates want to be the leader's friend—some more than others. Many believe that if they are on your good graces, then you will be lenient when they do wrong. You may even let things slide or look the other way. Second, they also expect favors. For example, if they are due for an annual performance evaluation, they expect a raise or maybe a promotion. They will never expect you to give them a bad evaluation. "We're friends, remember?"

The typical strategy for subordinates to develop that friendliness with you, the leader, is for them to, at first, be very nice and friendly—attentive. They go the extra mile in their work and maybe even bring you gifts. It's nothing too big early on—maybe some home-baked cookies or something they know you like. Then the gifts may get a little bigger. For example, I grew up in Kentucky, so I like the occasional sip of good Kentucky bourbon. I now have dozens of bottles of bourbon stored in a unique bar—all gifts. Every Christmas and birthday, my employees give me something nice. Certainly, I don't believe this is being done exclusively to brownnose. I think some do it because they are genuine and respect me (but maybe not?!). The point is that people have been and are always very nice to me when I have been the boss.

Another tactic to become your good friend is to lure you away from the office or work setting. "I've got a couple of tickets for the Indians game. Wanna go?" In a neutral environment, away from the workplace, the layers of authority and subordination melt away. You act more like yourself, and that boss barrier is broken down. You have suddenly become equals. You may let your guard down, talk about your feelings and thoughts. You start confiding and let loose your frustrations with people at work or about others. Perhaps you talk about controversial things like politics. Maybe you even slip and talk bad about other employees. You begin to develop closer bonds with those who work for you, and now they think you are their friend. They now know you on a personal level because you've shared your emotions and maybe a secret. They may start to believe they know how you think about things. It effectively weakens your authority when your employees know how to manipulate you into getting what they want. Be careful!

EMOTIONAL CONFLICT AND DECISIONS

There is emotional conflict in dealing with friends when you are a leader. As a boss, am I the best person to deal with a conflict arising with my best employee who is also a great friend? The answer is a big *NO*. You are now biased and may indeed show favoritism. Always remember that a leader of any company, department, or shift is always under the microscope. People are always watching to see how you are going to handle things. If they see you let things slide for your friend but not for others, your leadership significantly weakens. Consequently, if they see that you are tough, it could strengthen that leadership, but you certainly will lose a friend.

Just like nepotism rules, it is better if you do not make close friends at the workplace. It will put you in a bind. If you do, then be aware of the potential consequences.

Food for thought

Leaders should refrain from having close relationships at work, whether it involves close friends or family. You could find yourself in an emotional dilemma that could undermine your leadership if you make a favorable decision for your friends or relatives. Have you been in this position? How did you handle it?

CHAPTER 16

DON'T WEED EVERY GARDEN

"What is a weed? A plant whose virtues have never been discovered."

—Ralph Waldo Emerson

Weeds in a garden can injure or prevent a desired crop from growing on cultivated ground. But weeds are not always bad or useless to have around. Coffee bean bushes I observed at a Tanzanian coffee plantation were embedded in nests of thick weeds. There were so many weeds that it was difficult to find the coffee bean plants. I later discovered that this was done intentionally so that beneficial insects, living in the weed beds, eat and destroy the insects harmful to the coffee bean plants.

WEEDS AND BAD GUYS

Although some people in your workforce may seem like weeds, not the most stellar or effective, they may nevertheless have significant usefulness. We sometimes call them "bad," as in bad workers or bad bosses. It can be a relative description (in terms of how bad) and often depends on perspectives. For example, rich folks thought Robin Hood, the legendary heroic outlaw depicted in English folklore, was a bad guy because he stole from them. Yet the poor, who benefited from his crimes, thought he was a wonderful man.

Many good guys have bad guys as their pals because they balance each other—good cop/bad cop, *The Odd Couple*'s Felix (neat and good) and Oscar (disheveled and sometimes bad), *The Lion King*'s Simba (good lion) and Scar (bad lion). The point is that we need weeds and bad people around to balance out the good ones.

In leadership, it is important to recognize "bad" for what it really is. A person's opinion of someone as bad may not be accurate. They may just not like them much; it is an opinion and not a fact. Always ask yourself who is calling whom bad and why. It may not be real, or an unbiased assessment of their work. Make the judgment yourself.

Leaders will often get secondhand information about how wicked certain people are. "So-and-so just doesn't know what he's doing! He's just evil!" Top leaders are constantly barraged by tattletale employees letting them know who, in their ranks, is bad. Perhaps these "bad" people are great workers, but there is jealousy among their colleagues or subordinates. There is often much intrigue and many plots and subplots in a typical workplace. Who needs daytime soaps?

Was Saddam Hussein really a bad guy? Yes, to our Western values, he was a tyrant, a bully, and a madman. The media told us how evil this man was. We did not share his cultural values, but the region was relatively stable from major conflicts until he was deposed. Suddenly, a mass of other bad guys—many worse than Saddam—emerged and put the country into complete chaos. This is one reason we do not want to weed out all bad guys. Sometimes, they are good to have around and are useful. Balance is always important in any workplace.

I once knew a high-level supervisor who was a good person, but people deemed him a bad guy because he always demanded excellence and accountability. For many years, I was urged to fire, demote, and transfer him. He was everything I was not: He was detail-oriented, he kept tabs on subordinates, and he made sure things got done. I was looked on as a "nice" guy, but he was "bad." So, there was a sort of equilibrium—a homeostasis—that occurred between our working styles. It worked well, and I resisted everyone urging me to fire him. Then, one day, he made a mistake and was fired. His absence created immediate chaos. Everyone was, in an instant, *liberated*, and they came out of the woodwork to cause trouble and violate rules. It was a nightmare, and I had no way to control things. I lost my "bad guy" partner and the yin and yang balance went awry. This is why we don't always want to weed every garden!

A PARABLE

This concept of not weeding every garden can be seen in the following biblical passage:[1]

> Another parable put he forth unto them, saying, the kingdom of heaven is likened unto a man which sowed good seed in his field:
>
> But while men slept, his enemy came and sowed tares among the wheat, and went his way.
>
> But when the blade was sprung up, and brought forth fruit, then appeared the tares also.
>
> So the servants of the householder came and said unto him, Sir, didst not thou sow good seed in thy field? from whence then hath it tares?
>
> He said unto them, an enemy hath done this. The servants said unto him, Wilt thou then that we go and gather them up?
>
> But he said, Nay; lest while ye gather up the tares, ye root up also the wheat with them.
>
> Let both grow together until the harvest: and in the time of harvest I will say to the reapers, Gather ye together first the tares, and bind them in bundles to burn them: but gather the wheat into my barn.

This was part of a homily given at a recent Sunday Mass. It made me think about how this applies to leadership and everyday life events. As we know, life is full of bad things and bad people; it is not a perfect world, but we can learn from them—learn what not to do.

I have had my share of working with horrible employees at all levels, including professionals such as doctors and administrators. Sometimes, they are a necessity, and we may want them to grow with the wheat for a while. The parable suggests that if we pull the weeds early, we may bring up the good grain too, so we may want to let them grow together until the wheat matures. So, it may not be a good idea to always get rid of weeds or bad employees right away. They may help the good ones learn from them, and they may even become better employees themselves.

Food for thought

Learn what not to do from bad employees, bad processes, and bad events. You can let it go for a while so that good employees will learn, good processes will emerge, and amazing events will occur. Perhaps the weed may even become a flower someday. Have you ever kept a bad guy around . . . just to keep the balance?

CHAPTER 17

DON'T CARRY A BUNCH OF STUFF

"The shortest way to do many things is to do only one thing at a time."

—**Mozart**

Whenever I vacation near a beach, I eagerly wake up early—long before the sun even has the chance to rise—to go for a nice leisurely walk along the shoreline. Without the noisy chatter of people, I hear the calming sounds of ocean waves, watch gracefully soaring seagulls, feel a nice, gentle breeze against my skin, and smell the scent of the sea. It is oh so peaceful and calming.

On one occasion during my early 30s, I went for an early morning stroll with a camera around my neck, a dab of zinc oxide on my nose, a towel over my shoulders, flip-flops in one hand, and a small backpack in the other. I was ready to start my journey.

A gentleman wearing a pair of shorts and nothing else suddenly appeared before me. He slowly approached and, with a gentle smile, said, "Don't carry so much stuff when you walk; you cannot enjoy this marvelous existence of life," as he peered at the ocean and waved his arms toward the sky, sea, and sand. Then the apparition walked away, disappearing into the semidarkness. Rather perplexed and annoyed at having my spiritual feng shui disturbed, I did not pay much attention to his message.

Years into my leadership career and after having encountered many life experiences, I realized the chance encounter with the man on the beach provided me with words of wisdom that eventually led me to practice the concept of not putting so much on my plate at once. I have learned to focus on one thing at a time in order to do a good job with the task at hand.

TOO MUCH STUFF

As a young doctor, I used paper and pen to take notes so that I could remember what I was thinking when examining a patient's historical and physical condition, as well as my treatment plans and follow-up. They acted as simple notes for my own use in case the medical management didn't work and an alternative plan would be required. I gave my complete and undivided attention to my patients and their problems.

Eye contact, facial gestures, body language, and vocal tones were very important additional clues to help determine a diagnosis.

Jump ahead to the future, and I now find myself sitting behind a computer screen. I barely look at the person because I am so consumed with completing the electronic patient chart. I have become a data-entry robot for the insurance companies and the government payer. I must checkmark a preloaded set of physical, mental, and social condition questions. Then I input my physical findings, including pertinent negative findings. Finally, I must choose from a long list of preapproved diagnoses. In many cases, they expect me to make a diagnosis fit into their listed ones—the square peg in the round hole dilemma. Now, the eye contact is gone, deep listening is a thing of the past, and showing compassion and concern is nonexistent. My effectiveness as a compassionate and attentive medical doctor has been hampered by the requirements of excessive documentation.

Our American society and those who belong to the most recent generations are multitaskers. They can drive a car, listen to music, and text all at the same time. Doctors talk and listen to their patients but do not look at them. Kids study while playing video games or listening to loud music. People rarely sit and have a fully engaging conversation involving eye contact and other listening gestures. Even I have evolved to the point where I can type and carry on a conversation at the same time. I don't like it, and I'm not too good at focusing on either task.

Has society gotten so complex that we must do many things at once just to keep up? Certainly, technology has made it easier to do this, but at what cost to quality or workmanship and even lifestyle? Not only do we do too many things at once, but we own too many things too. According to Daniel Levitin, renowned psychologist, neuroscientist, and musician, among other incredible talents, "The average American owns thousands of times more possessions than the average hunter gatherer. In a real biological sense, we have more things to track than our brains were designed to handle."[1]

Another example of having too much on our plates is the dilemma of dual-income families. The generation after mine (Generation X) began to experience two-income family structures. Beginning in the 1960s, 75 percent of fathers were the sole breadwinner of the household, and only 25 percent had dual incomes. By the 1990s, 60 percent of households were dual-income families.[2] There are numerous articles that discuss and portray the damages that dual-income families incur on a family.[3] Yes, they make a lot more money and can have much material wealth, but there is evidence that families may suffer. According to the US Department of Health and Human Services, young children learn higher levels of self-esteem and self-confidence when both parents are available to care for them.[4] They also score better on cognitive development tests when one parent is at home full-time for longer periods before returning to work. Again, this is an example of dividing your time and attention resources and not fulfilling your responsibilities adequately.

WE NEED YOU BACK HOME, DR. D!

In *The Book of Awakening*, Mark Nepo tells a story about a man who is determined to paint his family room. He gets up early one morning and gathers his painting supplies—paint, mixing sticks, brushes, and a drop cloth. With the supplies tucked under his arms and a brush between his teeth, he grabs the open cans of paint with both hands and attempts to open the door. He suddenly loses his balance and then falls backward; red paint splatters all over him.

There was a time in my leadership experience when I was asked to serve on many community, state, and national boards, as well as other functions. I never declined, because I thought networking would be good for my organization. As a result, I was always away. One year, I traveled multiple times to San Diego; Washington, DC; and other destinations, rarely spending time at my office or home. At first, the traveling was fun and exciting, but it soon got wearisome.

Being away led to quite a few crises at the office. Many of the problems I had to solve were conducted from airports or even in the DC subway (I have always been amazed how my cell phone would work deep in those tunnels). One day, I was back at the office for a meeting when Margie, one of the division managers, simply stated, "We need you back home to fix our own problems, Dr. D. You need to quit trying to do so many things."

She was right. I was juggling too many board meetings, too many responsibilities, and too many office and public crises all at once—and not doing well at any one of them. I could not accomplish anything and often forgot to do things that were asked of me. I was carrying a bunch of stuff, and I could not get through the dang door without falling!

Leaders who carry too much will become incompetent and ineffective. Your leadership falters, and people begin to view you as weak and inadequate. Be careful not to fall victim to this dilemma. Please don't carry a bunch of stuff; rather, lighten the load and embrace the calm.

TWO-FRONT WARS

Not only does carrying a bunch of stuff often result in poor outcomes for the individuals, but it can also cause catastrophic events when viewed on the macro level. A two-front war is the dilemma of fighting battles or wars in two opposing fronts. Nazi Germany, during World War II, had to battle the Allied forces of Great Britain, France, Belgium, the Netherlands, and the United States on the Western Front and the Soviet Union on the Eastern Front. This was the second two-front war that century for the Germans, because the same scenario occurred during World War I, with the same result. The Germans lost the first war due to overwhelming collective resources (materials, personnel, technical knowledge) on the part of their enemies, while the second war was lost primarily due to the Germans running out of resources.[5]

The Vietnam War also illustrates a form of two-front war, the battles occurring in Vietnam and those with war protestors and the political rift domestically. The unpopularity of the war served to cause civil disobedience and unrest, with frequent riots and trouble. Even as a youth during those years, I was indoctrinated by the media that we were the bad guys and that we needed to pull out. The country could not sustain itself with such emotional and psychosocial turmoil. The United States eventually pulled out after much loss of life, resources, devastation, and destruction of the way America was.

This is yet another example demonstrating that we must focus on specific problems or issues one at a time instead of trying to do so many things at once. I have never met anyone who can multitask and do a great job at every task. One at a time with focus will improve the outcome and efficiencies.

DON'T SAY YES WHEN YOU MEAN NO!

How many times do we agree to do something that we really do not want to do? We usually agree because we don't want to disappoint someone. Leaders are at high risk for this because of the influence they can provide to others. Our positions in a company or society often put us in the spotlight, resulting in requests to serve in a variety of prominent positions or to attend functions.

Leaders naturally have a certain amount of power, and it makes us feel good to do something for others or to just belong to worthy causes. Frequently, however, we are just too tired to do one more thing or have already spread ourselves too thin. Or we may not even have an interest in the project we are being recruited for. Curiously, we almost always give in, even though we really don't want to. The trouble with this is the commitment does not come from the heart, so we won't do a good job, and people will be able to tell that the job was done halfheartedly. But it is hard for leaders to say no. We find ourselves often saying yes because we think we should.

An excellent metaphor to keep in mind is the story of the strangler figs. Plants such as banyans and vines that typically grow in tropical and subtropical areas have a sort of symbiotic relationship with the strangler fig. Early on, strangler figs provide support for the banyan tree, their host, to help it withstand strong winds and storms with their entanglements. But as they continue their "partnership," the figs commonly strangle the host trees by enveloping them and growing higher to reach the sunlight zone above the canopy. This eventually shades the host trees from the sun, resulting in their death.

People may do the same to leaders. Early on, we need their support to get things accomplished. As the company grows and the organization becomes more complicated, there are exponentially more people who continue to depend on your leadership. In addition, meetings, reviewing documents, giving advice, and making endless decisions eventually may have a stranglehold on you. Much like the fig, it can destroy the host—you! Like the fig tree parable, also know that sometimes these stranglers can save you by providing support in bad storms, so it's okay to say yes every once in a while, just not all the time. It is important to say no when you really mean no. Always remember to not carry too much stuff!

AS TASKS INCREASE, GOOD LEADERSHIP DECLINES

Doing a lot, having a lot, and spreading ourselves too thin does not equate to good leadership, nor does it result in good outcomes. Good and effective leadership is inversely proportional to carrying a bunch of stuff. Leaders need to have a clear, uncluttered mind so their decision can be accurate and focused; spreading yourself thin will never result in meaningful accomplishments. Remember that leaders are supposed to be the big-picture person, the visionary. How are we able to focus on the future when we are constantly being dragged down by many petty issues or so many minor tasks? On numerous occasions, I have found myself in positions where I am carrying too large a burden and cannot finish anything worthwhile. We always end up failing when that happens.

Food for thought

Do one thing at a time and do it well. Don't overload yourself. Leaders need to navigate around the solitary lighthouse and not the city lights. If you are a multitasker, try to focus on a specific task until it is done or at a good stopping point. The outcome will be better.

CHAPTER 18

DON'T BE A SAWBONES

"Chiropractors discover the underlying issues, instead of treating the surface symptoms."

—**Wellnessmediaresources.com**

I received a frantic call from my mom one day. It was one of many such calls in the past few days not long after celebrating her 60th birthday. Convinced she only had days to live because she's "old" now, she kept calling her doctor son, asking about a variety of medical conditions that have bad endings.

This call began a little differently. Her voice was more urgent, and she seemed afraid. In her not-so-fluent English, she exclaimed, "Ronald, I go to doctor today, and he say I got cancer! He want to do surgery next week. He said emergency!"

Mom had a recent bout with a nasty case of seasonal allergies and had been experiencing some frontal headaches and lots of postnasal drainage. She was referred to a local ENT (a specialist in the ears, nose, and throat) for further evaluation, including a CT[1] scan of the sinus areas. The ENT apparently informed her that she had some sort of cancer in her mouth.

I calmed Mom down and told her that I would call the doctor and try to get more information. She didn't believe me when I told her that I thought the doctor was wrong and that she probably would not need surgery. She got mad at me for not caring about her like a good son should.

The ENT, Dr. Bennett,[2] was pleasant when he returned my call. He explained that there was a small cystic lesion on my mom's soft palate and that he had done a CT scan confirming it was cancerous. That was odd to me because I had seen this lesion in her mouth years ago. She had informed me at the time that she had had it since early childhood—"as long as I remember." Years later, while I was in medical school, I "diagnosed" it as a dermoid cyst—a benign lesion found in both children and adults. It was probably congenital, and I never gave it another thought.

I did not tell Dr. Bennett that I'm also a doctor; I was calling as a son and didn't even think about identifying myself as a physician. I asked, "Does the CT scan show any localized boney invasion?" I knew that if the boney areas around the lesion were destroyed or lytic (eaten up), it could indicate a cancerous process. I gave him a bit more history about Mom and indicated this lesion had been in her mouth for years. I then asked, "How do you know it is not just a benign dermoid cyst?"

He did not answer right away, and after a few seconds, he became verbally aggressive. With a harsh voice, he asked, "Who do you think you are, questioning my diagnosis? Do you think you can get medical knowledge from just watching a few TV shows? Everybody thinks they're doctors these days. Let me give you a piece of advice, son. You don't ever question a real doctor's judgment and expertise. If your mom doesn't have this surgery right away, she's gonna be pushing up daisies and weeds from six feet under in a month!" Then he hung up! A rather crude statement, I thought.

This doctor was truly a sawbones! He jumped to an immediate conclusion and wanted to cut out the "cancer" right away.

I called the Cleveland Clinic's ENT department right away and asked to speak to a physician about this case. He was polite and asked to see my mom. After a few minutes of questions for the history, examining her completely, and reviewing the CT scan films, the Cleveland doctor made the diagnosis of chronic sinusitis needing to be treated with a course of antibiotics and saline nasal spray. He stated that the lesion on her soft palate was a benign dermoid cyst, probably congenital. No horrific surgery for her! Mom was relieved that she didn't have cancer but knew there must be something else wrong with her because "she's now 60 years old."

WHAT IS A SAWBONES?

Sawbones is another one of those slang terms my father-in-law liked to use regularly when describing physicians, especially the bad ones. He often concluded that many doctors wanted to "cut out" the problem rather than getting to the root of the situation.

Historically, the term was thought to have originated to describe US Civil War doctors who commonly performed amputations on the battlefield. Before the advent of antibiotics, one of the primary means of treating infected wounds was through amputation. The danger of gangrene developing from even the slightest cuts often had surgeons cutting off extremities or limbs to avoid sepsis. Wounds were then often cauterized (burned) with heated pokers.[3]

My mom's ENT doctor is a great example of jumping to conclusions and taking care of the superficial problem but not investigating further to look for root causes of the cyst. He immediately wanted to cut it out.

LOOK FOR THE UNDERLYING PROBLEMS

A basic tenet of understanding a patient's medical problem is to always look for the underlying problem. Superficial problems are symptoms of a disease. Get rid of the disease, and your superficial problems will go away. There are many practitioners I see today who immediately treat the symptoms or the obvious physical findings. The patients ultimately find themselves being treated with multiple medications and never get better.

A good medical example is the management of hypertension. There are multiple causes for high blood pressure, but I often see doctors treat the high numbers rather than identifying the underlying problems, such as kidney disease, vascular problems, or even a hormonal issue.

In business, the informational technology world seems to always be a patchwork of fixes. (It probably seems that way to me because I don't understand it!) Over the years, I have spent millions of dollars trying to get an IT system that runs smoothly without glitches. I have yet to have this luxury. Whenever there is a problem, the IT technician will make an adjustment or change a program or even change servers, and then it's okay, but soon, another problem occurs and, later, yet another. It never ends!

I always ask, "Why don't you look at the root causes instead of patching it?"

The answer is always the same: "The system wasn't set up properly. That's why you're having these problems!"

Okay, then why don't we reset the system—properly?

This principle of looking for and fixing underlying problems applies to just about any obstacle and not just the field of medicine or business. Identifying and addressing the core problems is immensely important for any leader of any organization to become successful. As another example we are all familiar with, employee issues are sometimes rampant in organizations, but if the underlying infrastructure of better hiring practices, properly vetting the candidates, better orientation, exemplary training, and continuing education were identified and practiced, then the problem would not exist. Look for, find, and take care of underlying problems that create the superficial problems. Don't always revert to the knife.

Food for thought

Superficial problems or issues are typically a result of deeper problems. Fix the underlying problem, and all your superficial problems will go away. Have you ever dug deeper at a problem? To solve most problems, it's best if you find and fix the underlying problem.

CHAPTER 19

DON'T IGNORE CRICKETS THAT LIVE IN WALLS

"I wish I had the power to
ignore you like you ignore me."

—**Unknown**

One of our dentists, Dr. Kiljoy,[1] complained about a loud cricket noise coming from the walls of her office. It was such an annoyance that she asked the office manager, Steve Fixit, to investigate. He quickly assessed and determined that it was indeed coming from inside the walls—between the drywall—and assured her that the insect would soon die and that it would be the end of the problem. Not satisfied, Kiljoy continued her rampage about this creature living in her walls.

The incessant complaints soon got to be such a joke around the office that people just shrugged and went about their work. A few days later, Kiljoy came to work and found a huge dead cricket lying on top of her desk. She screamed and ran out, yelling about harassment and a lawsuit. Fixit laughed and ignored her—even made more jokes, adding to the tension.

The issue reached the executive department, where after a brief investigation, it was discovered that two staff members had played a joke with the dead cricket. The dentist, now even more infuriated, proclaimed that she would file a suit against the organization for creating a hostile work environment. She also demanded the two pranksters be fired. The upper management, subsequently, spent almost an entire day pulling the pieces together and launched its own investigation so that an amicable resolution could be had. The two pranksters apologized to Dr. Kiljoy, who did not accept it immediately; however, the next day after the CEO spoke with her, the apology was accepted.

Another day went by before the noise from the wall ceased. After that, the cricket was never heard from again. All's well that ends well, right? Well, considering direct and indirect costs of the investigation and the time lost, the company paid over $4,000 to deal with this issue. The point of this story: Nip it in the bud! There are no problems small or large that should be ignored, especially when it is a personal work problem such as this one.

This practice is followed in larger companies as well. Consider the concept used by Toyota called *jidoka* (automation with a human touch).[2] *Jidoka* is a complicated word to translate from Japanese. It has several meanings, but the primary concept is that a process stops automatically if there are any irregularities detected by machines or humans.[3] Any assembly line worker can push a button to stop the entire assembly process if a problem is discovered. This method fixes any problems, even the smallest issues, before more defective production continues. The idea can be borrowed and used in any process, whether it involves manufacturing or service production. This scenario illustrates that when leaders empower frontline workers to make decisions when, perhaps, the quality of the product may be jeopardized, it can result in improved efficiencies, greater employee satisfaction, and improvement to the bottom line.

Sometimes, it's not the seemingly insignificant size of the immediate problem that matters but, rather, the resulting bigger issue it creates. Every problem needs to be taken seriously, even crickets in walls.

Food for thought

Always nip problems in the bud! Think of a time when you kept letting small problems go, but it kept getting larger until it was out of control.

CHAPTER 20

DON'T BE STINGY WITH KINDNESS

"Kindness? It may strike us as absurd to even approach the subject: Our world is full of violence, war, terrorism, devastation. And yet life goes on precisely because we are kind to one another."

—Piero Ferrucci

I was about to pull the Mastercard out of my wallet when the waitress, clearing the table, said with a smile, "Your dinner has been taken care of, and you owe nothing."

I was momentarily stunned. My daughter Abbey and I had just spent two days on top of Mt. Baker, in Washington State, and had made our way to Burlington—a small town about an hour's drive from the base of the mountain. There, we stopped at Bob's Burgers and Pub for our traditional post-climb dinner. Spread across our table were big, fat, juicy burgers, an ice-cold beer for me, a tall bottle of Coca-Cola for Abbey, steak fries, and two decadent desserts. It was a nice respite for our dirty, tired, and hungry bodies. Lugging around 40–50-pound backpacks on rocky and icy paths while treading in cramponed mountain boots is certainly no easy task and can burn thousands of calories in a single day. We used it as a great excuse to pig out and eat delicious, heart-attack-risk food.

As I looked at the large amount of food we had ordered, my mind raced, trying to determine who paid for the dinner. My wife? Friends? Perhaps our mountain guide. I wondered who I knew in Burlington, Washington. No one! But even if I did, no one knew we were here at Bob's.

So I asked, "Who paid for our dinners?"

The waitress hesitated, as if to protect the benefactor.

Although I had made it my own tradition some time ago to occasionally pay for strangers' meals, I had never been on the receiving end of this act of kindness until now. I was suddenly in high spirits. Someone would really do this for me? How kind! With so much negativity around us these days, my belief in the goodness of humankind was instantly restored.

The waitress wouldn't tell me his name but said that a gentleman who'd sat directly behind us wanted to pay for our dinners, since we seemed to be very nice people.

Wow, how powerful is that? It is kindness in the purest sense, where there are no ulterior motives, no boasting, and nothing expected in return. A man used his personal resources to pay for two strangers' meals. Maybe he felt sorry for us because of our ragged appearance. Or maybe it just made him feel good to be kind.

WHY KINDNESS

In Piero Ferrucci's extraordinary and poignant book, *The Power of Kindness*, His Holiness, the Dalai Lama, writes the preface, explaining the importance of kindness to the human soul:

> Kindness and compassion are among the principal things that make our lives meaningful. They are a source of lasting happiness and joy. They are the foundation of a good heart, the heart of one who acts out of a desire to help others. Through kindness, and thus through affection, honesty, truth, and justice toward everyone else, we ensure our own benefit.[1]

I believe the most incredible act of kindness is to do for or say nice things about someone you know nothing about. In my opinion, that is the purest form of kindness, because it does not matter why you are doing it. There is no self-gain or intent involved, and the chance that you will ever see the person again is very low. It is just something you do out of the absolute kindness of your being.

In the article "Connect, Then Lead," Harvard Business School's Amy Cuddy and her coauthors suggest that behavioral science shows that projecting "warmth" is the key to having influence.[2] Leaders who have warm personalities come across as kind and are more effective than people who lead with toughness. Kindness and warmth accelerate trust[3] and will encourage followers to respect and appreciate their bosses, creating more harmonious working conditions.

Although I have seen people use kindness to get things or favors from others, the act of kindness should never be a quid pro quo event.

It can be used as a powerful tool to build your integrity and self-worth to others. It develops trust and belief in the leadership. A leader who exemplifies kindness is much more likely to breed happiness, contentment, and productivity in the work environment.

We have all experienced the powerful effects on our emotions when we are kind to others. There is a feeling of euphoria, a happy high. In a 2016 systematic review of the scientific literature conducted by researchers from the University of Oxford and Bournemouth University, 21 studies proved that being kind to others makes us happier.[4] In addition, research from the University of Warwick revealed that happy people are 12 percent more productive at work than unhappy people.[5] The Oxford study showed that research does not distinguish between kindness toward family and friends and that toward strangers. Furthermore, the study reported that targeted (purposeful) kindness rather than indiscriminate (random) kindness may have a greater effect on happiness.[6] This suggests that targeted, planned, and purposeful kindness is as or more important than an impulsive and random act of kindness. This becomes a powerful tool for both leaders and followers.

PURPOSEFUL KINDNESS

Purposeful or intentional acts of kindness focus on seeking out and appreciating those you tend to overlook or take for granted. My attempt at this has been to use fundamental kindness through giving and recognition. I send birthday and gift cards to my staff. I write personal birthday greetings and thank them for their hard work. I give welcome cards to new employees and congratulations notes on their work anniversaries. I even send gifts and recognition cards to employees' family members for life events and accomplishments, such as graduating from high school, college, or even preschool, and personalized gifts for new babies (cute onesies or teddy bears with their names on it). I believe these actions show sincere kindness and gratitude that steers all of us toward better trust, respect, and gratitude between leaders and followers.

Purposeful kindness also comes from simple but conscious acts, such as intently listening to what people have to say, speaking to others with respect, being courteous, smiling, holding the door for others, helping and supporting people to accomplish things, and teaching them skills or helping to solve problems with them.

I have found that taking time to listen to or help mentor someone is a remarkable gesture of kindness. You may not always have a solution for the problem, but just by listening or mentoring, you have demonstrated compassion, interest, human warmth, and caring. The person may feel better and may even come up with their own solution. Leaders who listen to their staff will make responsive changes and will improve the quality of their workforce and will therefore improve productivity and quality of life.

Remember: Kindness is a two-way street. What you sow, you will reap.

Food for thought

Practicing purposeful kindness through the giving of yourself and resources such as time, teaching, helping, and listening will create a happier and more productive working and life environment. Practice kindness today. Buy someone's meal, or tell a stranger to have a good day.

CHAPTER 21

DON'T NEGLECT YOUR HEALTH

"If you don't have your health,
you have nothing."
—John N. Cernica, PhD

My father-in-law told me a story about a girl he dated while attending Carnegie Mellon University. It was during the early 1950s, when he was working on his engineering PhD. Judy[1] was an heiress to a wealthy family whose grandfather had founded a major international company based in Pittsburgh. She introduced my future father-in-law to her father after an outing one evening. Sadly, the patriarch of this extravagantly wealthy family was in poor health and bound to a wheelchair. He took a liking to my father-in-law and showed him around his cavernous house, including the many taxidermic trophies he had acquired during his youth. At one point on the tour, he suddenly stopped and waved his right hand around a stately room, declaring, "You can see all the wealth I have, but you know what I really have? Nothing! I have nothing because I have poor health. Always remember: Without good health, you have nothing."

HISTORY AND LEADERS

Bill O'Reilly, in his book *Killing England*, described King George III's health maladies. King George was the monarch who pushed the war effort against the colonists in their quest for independence from England. During the height of the war, he began to exhibit mental health symptoms, including disjointed thought processes and flight of ideas. His behavior eventually led to violent and manic episodes, resulting in confinement to a straitjacket. The war effort was in shambles, and the greatest army in the world suffered defeat at the hands of untrained and poorly armed farmers and peasants.[2]

There was no victory because the leadership had failed. King George's declining health led to a disorganized, disjointed effort that was doomed. History attributed the king's behavior to hereditary porphyria and arsenic poisoning. Ironically, the arsenic was used as a sort of insecticide powder on his ceremonial wigs, as well as to treat his mental condition.

As leaders, it is vital that we keep ourselves in the best physical and mental condition possible. How do we lead when we are preoccupied with health problems? Think of the last time you had a bad cold or the stomach flu. You feel too sick to do anything, let alone lead a bunch of people.

An important point about leadership and health is that a good leader will know when they are incapable of performing up to high standards due to ill health and must simply let go. Shinzo Abe, the Japanese prime minster for eight years, resigned because of a painful intestinal condition, ending his rule after he held the top job longer than anyone else.[3] It takes courage to step down from a powerful position, and it is an example of sacrificing personal desires, your ego, and your need for the greater good.

TIPS FOR GOOD HEALTH

This leads to the question of how leaders should maintain good health. First, there are many aspects of life that are uncontrollable. A great quote that I hear often is "People plan, and God laughs"; that fits well here. Certain health conditions cannot be helped, such as injuries from accidents, genetic disorders, and some mental illnesses and cancers.

Most chronic diseases are a result of poor health management, such as eating too much or eating inappropriately due to the inaccessibility of fresh foods and produce that may lead to diabetes or heart disease. And there is a significant amount of control that we do have, such as exercise, eating right, sleeping, practicing good safety precautions, and practicing spiritual relaxation.

To remain healthy takes a lot of work, dedication, and desire. It is the responsibility of not only leaders but also of the everyday Joe to keep fit and maintain their health. I sometimes wonder if it should even be a part of their job description.

I believe the key to good health is to have some daily, organized exercise sessions. These activities, along with good sleep habits, stress reduction strategies, and moderate food intake, are the focus strategies to keep healthy. I recently read a great blog by Dr. Sharon McDowell-Larsen of the Center for Creative Leadership, who teaches senior executives all over the world how to eat and exercise better to help them be fit to lead.[4]

She teaches that good health will contribute to good brain function, sustained energy output, and physical resiliency. She further explains that there are four interdependent pillars of good health.

- **Eat a nutrient-rich, health-promoting diet.** Eat a filet mignon instead of prime rib! You get good calories and low fat from the filet and the opposite for the rib!
- **Get adequate, quality sleep.** Seven to eight hours a day of straight sleep instead of interrupted sleep is best for you.
- **Engage in regular physical activity.** Do something at least daily. Make it a habit. Even a few sit-ups count!
- **Avoid turning pressure into stress.** Learn to meditate and stay calm. Remember to just let it go.

An important concept about the four pillars is that they are interdependent. For example, without adequate sleep, your exercise routine may suffer because you are too tired. Being too tired will affect your appetite, resulting in poor food choices, such as binge eating.

The four pillars emphasize that the importance of sleep and rest is the cornerstone. There are many reasons people have difficulty with sleep, such as excessive worrying, a lack of exercise, and too much alcohol. A simple strategy for better sleep is to go to bed earlier and at about the same time every night to take advantage of the melatonin spikes commonly noted around 10:00 p.m. to 3:00 a.m. Sleep time before midnight provides the deepest and most restorative sleep. A lack of sleep hurts our internal mechanisms of satiation—ghrelin, a hormone that increases appetite, goes up, and leptin, a hormone that suppresses appetite, goes down. This increases the likelihood of eating too much junk or calorie-rich foods. Eating nutrient-poor and calorie-rich foods, in turn, can hurt your sleep. This probably explains why most of my classmates in medical school became overweight! We were sleep deprived in all four years from studying many hours into the night, snacking on junk food, and not exercising.

The four pillars must work in concert with one another, where the whole is greater than the sum of the parts. For instance, if we neglect one, then the rest will not proceed properly. Take care of one, and this will improve your ability to take care of the others.

Dr. McDowell-Larsen states, "We often encourage leaders to 'win the morning, win the day.'" That is, start the day with some vigorous physical activity after a good sleep, and other healthy habits can result.

For me, I go to bed early and wake up early. I try to consume a low-carb diet and eat moderately. I reduce my stress load through exercise and meditation. I self-massage my neck, feet, face, hands, and wrist every morning. I take nice leisurely showers twice a week, and I do my own aromatherapy frequently. These routines give me a contented, relaxed lifestyle, and at 65, I have never been on chronic medications for anything. I am ready to go every single day, and I can often mentally outthink, physically outperform, and outlast any 20-year-old in my office.

I'm not bragging; it's just a result of lifetime fitness and discipline. After all, no leader wants to emulate King George's health habits!

Food for thought

To be an effective leader, keep yourself fit and healthy. It is your responsibility. Have you created a fitness plan for yourself? Check your blood pressure and heart rate every day. Keep an eye on your weight and exercise regularly.

CHAPTER 22

DON'T BE NICE

"No good deed goes unpunished."

—Lance Morrison, attorney

Mowing the lawn for a sick neighbor, giving money to charity, smiling a lot, and being approachable are all nice things to do. We show good manners by saying "yes, ma'am" and "no, sir." And it's nice to open doors for people. Women think men are nice if they see them playing with babies and doing baby talk. Being a leader gives us many opportunities to do nice things for people. Most leaders, I believe, want to be perceived as benevolent; they want to be liked. Sometimes, you want people to like you so much that you might go overboard or create unrealistic expectations. Be a bit cautious: The overniceness may backfire and could cause problems for both you as a leader and your employees, staff members, and direct reports.

TIME CLOCK STORY

When I became the head of my medical clinic, I had no business experience and understood very little of organizational behavior; I was a young doctor not far removed from medical school. The clinic began as a small mom-and-pop shop with only a few employees. Soon, it became one of those feel-good places to work because of the noble mission to help poor people get quality health care. It grew quickly to a dozen employees within a year.

One of the first actions I took, as a "nice" leader (but quite naive), was to eliminate the time clock. I thought that keeping track of when employees arrived and left was one of the dumbest inventions ever made. How do you measure quantity and quality of work based on a time measurement? Does time necessarily equate to more productivity and better quality? Certainly, I understand the importance of measuring time for the purposes of quantification so people can be paid fairly; however, in my mind, there is something wrong when you look at accomplishments in terms of time as opposed to successful completion of tasks and projects.

One day, I had a "brilliant" idea. Wouldn't it be nice to let my employees manage their own time? They are adults, after all, and I don't need to police every minute of their day. This experiment began well—much better than expected. My staff came in early and left late, often not even taking breaks or lunch. They were productive and happy. Niceness even spilled over to our patients. It became the perfect workplace, all because I was nice and probably a marvelous boss for coming up with this outstanding idea. My theory was working well.

The second week didn't go as well. I noticed some of my staff missing during different portions of the day. The remaining ones weren't smiling, and the laughter and cheeriness had gone extinct. When I asked where so-and-so was, I would get a grumpy reply: "Oh, they went on a McDonald's break. They said they'd be right back. That was about two hours ago." Then I would see the eye-rolling, indicating they had no idea when their colleague would return.

By the third week, things became worse. Many of my staff members were missing in action, leaving our patients without a doctor and nurse to see them. The employees who did stay were in bad moods and appeared angry, throwing things around and yelling at one another. Our patients were in worse moods and vocalizing it: "Where's everyone at? What kind of a doctor's office is this?" Moms, kids, the elderly, and adolescents were crowded in the waiting rooms, getting more and more upset because they had waited for hours with very poor or no service. No one escaped the horrible mood.

Less than a month after I started my experiment, I reimplemented the time clock. There were employees who thanked me for bringing it back. They had experienced chaos, and they did not like it. Most wanted the structure and rules so everyone would be treated fairly. Ironically, by trying to be nice, I inadvertently set my staff up for failure.

Imposing structure on your team isn't about not being nice; it is more about being fair, having a good plan, and not being naive. At the time, I was an inexperienced leader, and I wanted to be popular, thinking that if I was, my staff would do anything for me. This is not always true. The better perspective is to be fair and honest. Be prepared, and create solid foundations through good policies and planning for your infrastructure. Like kids, people do much better in a structured, fair, and honest environment rather than a free-for-all environment. You can be a nice leader, but just be a smart one too!

Food for thought

Be careful not to mix up being nice and naive. Be nice, but also be smart. Have you ever been burned by being nice?

CHAPTER 23

DON'T LOOK THE OTHER WAY

"Stupid is as stupid does."

—**Forrest Gump**

"Let me stir your coffee with my special stick!"

After brewing coffee in the clinical break room, a male medical provider allegedly made this declaration to a female nurse as he gyrated his hips. This incident, along with other crude comments and alleged activities, resulted in a costly and time-consuming sexual harassment lawsuit for my clinical organization.

Not only were there enormous financial consequences, but significant business processes suffered too. I and others on the executive level were forced to spend countless hours discussing the case with attorneys, taking us away from valuable projects and other important matters. On the staff level, employees were distracted by rumors and gossip about a sexual harassment lawsuit. Publicly, it was embarrassing for me to attend community meetings where someone might ask me how the lawsuit was going.

At the end of this two-year ordeal, everyone lost. The accusers settled for a very small fraction of their initial demand. It cost my nonprofit health-care program hundreds of thousands of dollars to defend, and my patients were unable to receive timely care. I am certain there were marketing and public relations damages. As the saying goes, the lawyers were the only ones who made out.

Harassment of any kind is a serious allegation that all leaders should be aware of and a real and constant threat. There is no reason anyone should engage in harassment and inappropriate behavior. Nor should this behavior be condoned or swept under the rug. Comprehensive trainings of new hires, regular updates, continuing education, and immediate dismissal of offenders through zero tolerance are necessary and effective tools for prevention. Otherwise, it can have devastating ramifications for your business—small or large.

UNDERSTANDING SEXUAL HARASSMENT

Sexual harassment is a form of the broader category of harassment and occurs even in the smallest organizations. It is typically defined as unwanted comments, requests, or actions of a sexual nature that are made a term or condition of employment, that are used to interfere with a worker's performance, or that are severe or pervasive enough to create a hostile working environment.[1] These activities are considered illegal sex discrimination in violation of Title VII of the Civil Rights Act of 1964 and are enforced by the Equal Employment Opportunity Commission (EEOC).

Intentional and sometimes unintentional sexually offensive acts or verbal statements by an offender can be construed, reconfigured, twisted, and distorted to create an apparent environment of evil and vicious doings by the wrongdoer. For example, sexual jokes may seem innocent to the offender but may be received in an ill manner by the victims. We may see both genders in playful sexual bantering, laughing and seemingly enjoying the exchange, only for it to later be perceived as offensive and to eventually result in allegations of sexual misconduct. This can include complaints from others within an organization who witness sexual harassment in their workplace but were not the direct target of it.

Although bad behavior is not exclusively perpetrated by males, as may be implied by the opening of this chapter, the statistical data support that most harassment or offenses are initiated and perpetrated by males against females.[2] According to data reported by the EEOC for 2017, the main federal agency responsible for receiving and investigating workplace sexual harassment charges, 16.5 percent of the sexual harassment charges received by the agency were filed by men. The remaining 83.5 percent charges were filed by women. This, however, does not establish how much more likely women are to experience sexual harassment; it only indicates how much more likely they are to report sexual harassment to the EEOC than men.[3]

It is important for leaders to be aware that men, too, are vulnerable to sexual harassment at the workplace; however, men may be reluctant to report victimization due to embarrassment or the feeling that to do so is an unmasculine act.[4]

Despite these research findings, it is still important to know that the more commonly reported paradigm is the male perpetrator and female victim. Either way, it is wrong to cross the line by assuming the opposite sex enjoys advances or crude jokes or even touching. Leaders need to protect all individuals through assuring safe working areas and through the development of a respectful working force.

RAMIFICATIONS OF SEXUAL HARASSMENT

No one gains and everyone loses when sexual harassment occurs in any setting. Poor outcomes are experienced by victims, the harasser, the employer, other employees, the business, and even the community.

The consequences of sexual harassment can be devastating, especially for women. Researchers have found that women who experience workplace sexual harassment may be more likely to have financial stress, lower job satisfaction, and higher turnover rates than women who don't experience sexual harassment.[5] For male victims, whether in the form of verbal or physical abuse, harassment had negative effects on job satisfaction and psychological well-being.[6] Both women and men may experience long-term effects and may never recover fully.

Employers may lose employees due to the hostile environment that is created by these types of offenses, especially if their current employees feel as though it could happen again or if they perceive retaliation against their friends or coworkers on either side of the complaint. They may not want to work for such a troubled company. Not addressing the problem may further strain employer–worker relationships and could even damage the reputation of the company. If the company did nothing to help the victim—or, worse, shielded the harasser—their public image may suffer. Clients, stockholders, and employees may not want to have anything to do with the company or their business.[7] Getting ahead of the problem by immediately investigating and dealing with the allegations is a good first step to help lessen the potential consequences to the company.

Finally, the harasser could face serious consequences, including reprimand, demotion, or termination. In addition, if the conduct rises to the level of sexual assault, the harasser may even face criminal charges.

DEAL WITH IT, RIGHT AWAY!

A sealed envelope with my name—"Dr. D"—precisely printed and centered on the front was left on my chair one morning before I even got to work. Expecting a busy day and not in a mood to read what was probably yet another employee complaint, I tossed it on my desk, then made my way to see patients, intending to read it later.

Sometime around midday, I read the letter. By the time I got through the first paragraph, I was appalled at the graphic nature of some of the details. The letter was from a female nurse, who described the vulgar language, lewd acts, and extremely inappropriate behavior of one of our top female doctors.

Repulsed by what I read, I was sickened to my stomach, and I am sure my skin was ashen. The nurse ended her letter complaining that she and the other female staff in the clinical areas felt that this doctor was sexually harassing them and demanded that I take some action. Failure to do so would result in legal action against the organization.

This was quite a shock. Not knowing how to deal with the situation, I decided to ignore it for the moment. I was not thinking clearly. I was confused by the fact that my best doctor was somehow involved in such despicable behavior, and it made me upset. Maybe it would go away. I left the letter on my desk and went home.

The next morning, awakening from a restless sleep, I realized I had better run this past our legal counsel. After I had given him the details of the letter over the phone, there was a long, silent pause on the other end.

I waited and finally asked, "Are you there?"

The attorney sighed deeply and then replied, "Ron, there are two things you need to do. First, shut down the organization. Second, you need to resign immediately!"

I was stunned. What was he talking about? Finally, it dawned on me that he was trying to impress on me how serious this situation was.

I said, "Okay, I get it. Let's roll our sleeves up and tackle this!"

It took several weeks of investigative work by professionals, thousands of dollars, and hundreds of hours of my time to unravel the goings-on in the clinical areas. It was much worse than I thought and included intimidation and a clinical culture marred with sexual innuendos and even bribery of employees. It resulted in the doctor's termination, and, eventually, almost the entire support clinical and clerical staff were either dismissed or quit. The organization took almost three years to recover after that.

As they say, I would be lying if I said I had never suspected that this doctor was up to no good. She was quite professional-looking—well put together, as some described her—but she had a truck driver's foul-mouthed vernacular and did not use any discretion when it came to sexual, racial, and ethnic matters. Still, I tried convincing myself they must be thinking about someone else or making this up.

Leaders should not look away from any form of harassment. My failure and poor logic initially led me to believe that I needed her to continue to be a top-producing doctor and my chief medical officer, so I initially looked the other way. Thank God I got my senses back by the next morning and forged ahead to do the right thing.

IMPORTANT FACTS LEADERS MUST KNOW ABOUT SEXUAL HARASSMENT

The following facts about sexual harassment at the workplace, referenced from the online article "How to Prevent Sexual Harassment in the Workplace" from the Balance Careers website,[8] are essential knowledge for leaders. Awareness, understanding basic rules, and following established processes are the keys to a successful outcome.

Harassment can be perpetrated by same-sex individuals. Anyone associated with the employee's workplace can be accused of sexual harassment. Victims of sexual harassment can be bystanders as well. They do not have to be the actual target of the harassment. A good example is one where a supervisor may have a sexual relationship with a direct report. The direct report's colleagues and other staff members may be treated in a less favorable manner by the offending supervisor. This can be construed as a sexual harassment situation.

The workplace sexual harassment policy should advise potential victims, in the case of harassment, that they should ask the perpetrator to stop and that the advances are unwanted and unwelcome.

The victim should use the recommended procedures outlined in the sexual harassment policy of their employer.

During and following an investigation of a harassment complaint, no retaliation is permitted, regardless of the outcome of the investigation. The employer must not treat the employee who filed the complaint differently than other employees are treated or change his or her prior-to-the-complaint treatment.

To bring the point home, "Let me stir your coffee with my special stick" sounds like a harmless statement; however, it was hardly innocent. Lives and careers were damaged, and the collateral damage was significant. Take anything with the slightest suspicion of offense seriously and deal with it immediately.

Food for thought

Leaders need to be aware that bad things happen at the workplace. One of the most important responsibilities a leader must recognize is that they must keep inappropriate behavior, especially something like sexual harassment, at bay, and it must be nipped in the bud. Create an environment where everyone respects one another, regardless of gender, race, or creed. It is the right thing to do, and it will save everyone a lot of grief. Do you see sexual harassment activities occurring at the workplace? Do you have a sexual harassment policy at your place of business?

CHAPTER 24

DON'T HESITATE TO DELEGATE

"When you delegate tasks, you create followers. When you delegate authority, you create leaders."

—Craig Groeschel

Imagine my surprise when I came into my office one morning and found the COO crying. She appeared disheveled and upset, as if she had not slept all night.

I asked, "What's wrong, Betty?"

After I let her sob for a few more minutes, she finally replied, "I accidently pushed the wrong button on the new computer system and deleted an entire office's data. All the appointments and all the patient accounts just disappeared!"

I was a bit perplexed and did not quite understand. How do you erase an entire clinical site? She was not an IT systems person, but I thought it must not be easy to eliminate an entire facility's data. I had delegated to her the task of cleaning up the office's data to make the computer processing more efficient.

One of the most crucial tasks a leader must be able to perform is to acquire and develop the art of delegating. Although it seems obvious to delegate busy work, it is also important to delegate power to allow freedom of choice and decision-making. This creates buy-in from your staff, a sense of ownership, and improved self-esteem that will lead to efficient processes, happier customers, outstanding products, and better services. However, it is important for leaders to keep in mind that delegated tasks may not always come out as well as you expected.

Being mortified and suffering from severe temporary stress during this time taught Betty an important lesson about what not to do on the new computer system. When I learned about the error, my first question was "So, what did you learn by this mistake?"

Her reply: "I learned that if I don't know how to do something, I should delegate the task to someone who does and try to learn from them before I attempt it on my own."

We were never able to retrieve the entire lost data; however, when new data was input to replace the old, the information was cleaner, and our employees became more adept—including Betty—with the new system due to repetitive processes. It all ended well!

The art of delegation is not easy for many people, especially those who are high achievers or who have obsessive personalities. Often, the task of delegating may be hampered by a lack of capable personnel. You must develop an infrastructure of strong and adequate members for your team before any delegation can be achieved.

An important concept of delegation that some leaders have difficulty adhering to is to delegate not only tasks but also authority. Give them the power to make decisions and know that mistakes will be made. By granting authority, you create new leadership. For example, I had given Betty the authority to fix our computer information, and despite some setbacks, she ended up becoming an expert in that computer system, teaching many people how not to erase an entire medical site.

REASONS NOT TO DELEGATE

There are several reasons leaders may hesitate or refrain from delegating or may be overly cautious about who is tasked with what. Early on in my leadership experience, an incident hampered me from delegating. I had asked my secretary to make copies of a handout for a presentation. My instructions were to simply make 50 copies of the handout. When I passed them out and started my PowerPoint presentation, people were leafing through the handout, appearing confused. I was distracted and asked if there was a problem. It turned out that my secretary did not copy the backside of the handout because I did not instruct her specifically to copy both sides. I was afraid to delegate for a long time after that, because it was just not worth the trouble; I did everything myself.

Delegation is a tough act to perform for some leaders. Here are the more common reasons some leaders hesitate to delegate.

Job security

I have seen people in leadership and management positions who purposely hire subpar workers or who do not provide enough training to their direct reports in order to maintain a higher level of knowledge and power. This allows them to not feel threatened by a subordinate potentially replacing them. Certainly, leaders and managers like this have low self-esteem and should not be in leadership; however, it is a scenario I have witnessed numerous times over the years.

I can do it better and faster myself

I have often been guilty of this reason not to delegate. It's often faster and requires less effort for me to do the task than it would to take the time to provide detailed instructions to someone else. I ultimately end up doing most of the work myself. Besides, I know if I do it, I'll get better-quality work out of it and it will get done on time.

Territorialism

"It's mine, and I don't want anyone to touch it." This is territorialism. Like many of these reasons to avoid delegation, territorialism is a form of either efficiency or selfishness, depending on how you look at it. You want the project done your way and in your time, and delegating would require both trust and clear instructions.

Not getting credit

It was my idea, you might think, and my way to do it, but since I gave the task to someone else, they end up getting the credit. I deserve to get the credit for my work.

Fear of weakness

"I'm the leader and should know this stuff!" Some leaders think that delegating is a sign of weakness or may reveal an inability to complete the task. Their thinking may be that since they are the leader, they must know everything.

REASONS TO DELEGATE

In 2005, I was accepted to participate in a two-week health-care executive program at UCLA's Anderson School of Management. An intriguing story that one of the professors related was about Nordstrom's business model. The professor was a sitting member of Nordstrom's board of directors, and his wife loved their annual shoe sales; those facts made him very fond of the store. He described their mission statement: "Our mission is to continue our dedication to providing a unique range of products, customer service, and great experiences." An important goal of this mission is *to provide outstanding service every day, one customer at a time.*[1] Part of the company's culture was to allow every Nordstrom employee to have the power to make customer-related decisions.

Our speaker told us a story. In 1975,[2] a man purchased four snow tires at a tire shop but needed to return them several weeks later. When he pulled up to the tire shop where he thought he had purchased them, the shop had closed and had been replaced by a Nordstrom store. He decided to see whether Nordstrom would take the tires "back." After explaining his situation to a salesclerk, Nordstrom (a store that does not sell tires) allowed him to return the tires, and they even refunded his money.[3]

On the surface, this appears to be a very bad decision made by the salesclerk. However, the notoriety and repetition of the story as an example of great customer service have had some significant indirect revenue benefits, I am certain. Nordstrom is a testament to the importance of empowering employees and supporting the policies that inspire them to do what's best for customers. Frontline workers need the wiggle room to make snap decisions that benefit their customers.[4]

The following are some common reasons why leaders should delegate.

You don't know how it works

There are so many things I don't understand about computers that I just simply give the work to someone else to do. I don't really want to know how to do it, and I don't particularly care. Just understand what your ultimate end product should be, and assign it to someone who can do it faster and better than you can.

It's cheaper

My salary is higher than my secretary's. It would cost me $XXX to do the work myself but $X for my support staff members to do it. It makes sense to delegate.

Get a different perspective on task completion

There are always different ways to do things. If nothing else, it may be good to see how others will approach a problem and solve it differently from how you would have. Often, two heads are better than one!

Use it as a teaching tool

One of the roles of a leader is to teach. What better way to do this than to give a task and let someone work through it? Let them make mistakes!

The lack of time

Leaders are frequently obligated to meetings, reviewing documents, and making decisions. Sometimes, there are just not enough hours in the day!

It is not possible to be a leader of anything or anyone without assigning some of your burdens and tasks to others. Be sure to not hesitate to delegate.

Food for thought

You cannot do it all. Delegate, and make sure you delegate authority as well. Do you have trouble delegating?

CHAPTER 25

DON'T BE A ZOOKEEPER

"The wise leader does not intervene
unnecessarily. The leader's presence is felt,
but often the group runs itself.
Lesser leaders do a lot, say a lot, have
followers and form cults.
Even worse ones use fear to energize the
group and force to overcome resistance.
Only the most dreadful leaders
have bad reputations."

—**John Heider,** *The Tao of Leadership*

As mentioned in an earlier chapter, in the summer of 2018, my daughter Abbey and I went on a weeklong safari to the Serengeti and the Ngorongoro Crater. As dusk slowly blanketed the great plains, we spotted two female lions creeping slowly through the tall grass toward a lone zebra. Drinking peacefully at a shallow watering hole and unaware of the stalkers ready to pounce and snuff its life away, the unwitting zebra remained calm.

Suddenly, without warning, the two huge cats lunged toward their prey, snapping the zebra out of its tranquility as it dashed away. The intense drama was short-lived, as the zebra was able to outrun these predators; the zebra's stamina was significant, and the lions' quick bursts of energy did not last.

The palms of my hands, gripping the binoculars, were moist, and my heart pounded fast and hard. I shook my head in amazement and made a comment to our safari guide, Ahgri, about how the animals in American zoos never do anything except lie around and sleep all day. But, here, in this vast plain, the drama of life is never-ending.

Ahgri mused for a moment, and then, with his thick Swahili accent, profoundly stated, "That is because a lion cannot be a lion in a zoo. Someone gives it food, water, and shelter every day. They do nothing else. They have no life purpose, so they are no longer lions."

Similar metaphors can be used in so many everyday situations, including leadership and parenting. For example, helicopter parents are those who hover over their kids. They are hyper-involved in their children's lives and are so overwhelming with every move and decision for the child that these kids become handcuffed. Free-range parents are those who let their kids think and do independently. In theory, they let them make mistakes and learn from them, but many have the tendency to become lawnmower parents: They mow the kids down (instantly take over) at the first sign of trouble, so the kids remain safe and unhurt.[1]

Likewise, as leaders, we provide our employees with guidance through job descriptions, policies, and protocols. But we must refrain from doing the work for them. In both scenarios, they may make mistakes, get hurt, or even flounder, but if we never let them out of the cage, they may ultimately fail. Confinement restricts imagination and exploration. As parents and leaders, we must not micromanage but must support, teach, and give guidance. That is our job!

WORKERS DON'T LIKE BEING MICROMANAGED

When employees are micromanaged—when they are constantly monitored and controlled—they are not able to make a move without fear. The lion in the zoo is being micromanaged and has no say-so in where and how it lives. It does not decide when it eats; it does not even have to rely on its own wit and senses to survive. All of the lion's innate abilities have been taken away. It is no longer a lion. We certainly don't want our employees to no longer be employees.

In a survey conducted by Trinity Solutions and published in author Harry Chambers's 2004 book *My Way or the Highway*, 79 percent of respondents had experienced micromanagement leadership. Many, 69 percent, said they thought of changing jobs because of micromanagement, and another 36 percent did so; 85 percent said their morale was negatively affected.

In the workplace, micromanaging can have a tremendous effect on a company or business. It is a primary cause in triggering disengagement, because the message is "we don't trust your work or judgment." Disengagement often leads to absenteeism, costing a typical 10,000-person company $600,000 a year in salaries for days where no work was performed. The turnover costs of micromanagement for most sizable businesses can be in the millions every year.[2]

HOW MICROMANAGERS CAN AVOID MICROMANAGING

Good leaders do not micromanage; they teach. Recall the proverb "Give a man a fish, and you feed him for a day; teach a man to fish, and you feed him for a lifetime." We should not eviscerate people and take their natural abilities away by doing and thinking for them. They will never learn and grow.

Because I've been deemed a high achiever since childhood, I know that I am vulnerable to becoming a micromanager. Based on my 40 years of experience in leadership, I have used various strategies to help me overcome these undesirable characteristics. I often present the following in my leadership lectures for future doctors and public health leaders.

The 95-95-95 rule

Many leaders micromanage because either they are perfectionists or they have no faith in their staff. In their minds, there is no one else who can do that job as well as they can. A good solution is to play a mind game with yourself. If you can accept a 95 percent perfect performance 95 percent of the time, then you will micromanage 95 percent less.[3]

Have regular meetings

If you are a micromanager, set goals and have scheduled check-ins to determine progress. A leader who micromanages often has trust and control issues. To help manage that, hold weekly meetings to discuss progress and to minimize any anxiety about not having control.[4]

Focus on results

Leaders can easily get bogged down in the dredges of everyday activity. Entrenched in minutiae, micromanaging is one classic example that wreaks havoc on a leader's purpose and resources. Avoid it by simply homing in on the big picture: the results. When leaders are focused on outcomes rather than the people and processes that produce those outcomes, their efforts are better served.[5]

Review your own job description

What are the top two to three key things someone at your level of leadership should spend the majority of time on? Write down your answers and review it daily. Then focus on doing your job. Part of this includes ensuring your direct reports understand your expectations and that they have all the information, resources, and tools they need to do their jobs.[6]

Communicate openly

One of the surest ways to stop micromanaging is to have an open dialogue with all team members. A leader's staff may expect feedback on their work, but truly opening the door for them to regularly provide feedback to a manager will allow those team members to indicate what's working and not working, including a tendency to micromanage.[7]

Hire the best

Typically, leaders micromanage their employees because of a lack of trust in the employees' capability to perform. It is important to hire the best talent with the right capabilities so that you can be sure they will execute the job well. Once you have the best talent with the right capabilities in place, you can delegate with trust and ease up on the micromanager mentality.[8]

Interestingly, as mentioned in Chapter 24, I have worked with managers who purposely hired incapable people. They claim that it is job security, their mindset being that if they hired someone bright and capable, that person may end up taking their job.

Awareness, aversion, and alternatives

Being on the receiving end of micromanaging is demoralizing. The root cause of leaders who micromanage is fear. A good strategy for leaders is to use the three As. First, become *aware* of the source of fear. Now, being aware of the fear source, consciously move away from micromanaging by *averting* your behavior. Then find a better *alternative* to micromanaging.[9]

Experiment

Because micromanagers often lack trust, they could try an experiment with one person for one project that does not have much at stake. Give the right directions or instructions and set expectations, and then see if the results are satisfactory.[10] This may eventually help build their confidence and evolve out of the micro-managerial mindset.

Be a leader instead of a manager

Get out of the weeds. The key to not micromanaging is to let go of the details and trust your employees to handle them. When you shift from manager to leader, you expand your capacity by taking on more responsibility. Shift from doing the work to leading conversations and guiding others to do what needs doing.[11]

Vacation mode

Put yourself in vacation mode—in the mindset of someone who is leaving for vacation—every day. Think of the last-minute items that need to be completed before you go on a trip. It is typically hectic. You can use this strategy when you suspect you may be micromanaging or interfering. Handle the problems and projects closest to you that require your expertise. Leave the rest for your team; they have this.[12]

Don't respond too quickly to emails

If your typical response time for emails is quick, like two minutes, then wait half an hour. With that added buffer, by the time you respond, your employee might have already come up with the answer. When you micromanage, you enable learned helplessness of your team. The only way to break that is to allow them to reach the answer on their own, without you. Eventually, they will learn to come to you only for the bigger questions.[13]

Allow others to point out the habit

Make sure that your team knows that they can politely point out when you are micromanaging without fear of retribution. If you can catch yourself in the beginning, you can readjust and change direction.[14]

Not all micromanagers are the same. They become micromanagers for a variety of reasons. For example, new leaders have not learned what to manage, so they may get too involved. Experienced leaders may not know how to delegate, so they cannot let go. Some leaders lack reliable data. Other leaders are trying to manage poor performers. A few are simply mistrusting and need to compensate.

Ken Melrose, former CEO of Toro Company, makers of lawn-mower equipment, was a believer in the concept of servant leadership. He wrote in his 1995 book, *Making the Grass Greener on Your Side*, "Bit by bit, I came to understand that you lead best by serving the needs of your people. . . . You don't do their jobs for them; you enable them to learn and progress on the job."

In an interview with the Associated Press, he told them, "In the '70s at Toro, if you tried something new and it failed, you got canned. So not many people wanted to try anything new."[15] This helped create a cultural work environment where employees were afraid to try new things at the risk of losing their jobs.

We don't want our leaders to be zookeepers. We want a lion to have freedom and to let it live its life fulfilled. Similarly, we want our employees to do what they were hired to do: to be creative, to be good employees who contribute and grow to fulfill theirs and the company's needs. Don't put people into imaginary cages. If you do, they will never be allowed to be lions, because a lion cannot be a lion in a zoo!

Food for thought

Don't micromanage! Lead with a soft hand to stir the imagination and allow creativity. Let workers be workers and lions be lions!

CHAPTER 26

DON'T AVOID DIFFICULT CONVERSATIONS

"When we avoid difficult conversations,
we trade short-term discomfort for
long-term dysfunction."

—**Peter Bromberg**

Addressing problems as quickly as possible is a hallmark of medical practice. As a physician, I understand preventive practices and that early intervention saves lives. We see this in everyday life as well. For example, as a society, many of us eat too much and do not get enough exercise. This leads to obesity, which results in chronic diseases, such as diabetes, heart disease, and even certain cancers. These diseases eventually become death sentences for many. If we address our overeating and start exercising at an earlier age, perhaps many of these problems could be avoided. This applies to smaller situations too. If we have a small superficial cut, for example, we should take care of it by washing the wound with soap and water, then applying a topical antibiotic ointment to the cut area—maybe even applying a bandage. If we don't do this, the cut could turn into an infection. This infection could then spread to underlying boney areas, requiring vigorous IV antibiotic treatment, sometimes in a hospital. It is possible that if this wound is not managed properly, the infection may even get into the blood, causing sepsis and even death.

This concept of early intervention and prevention applies to many situations in life, including the workplace. One of the most avoided interventions is to initiate a difficult conversation with a coworker or employee. No one likes confrontations or discussing negative subjects. Leaders in any organization must, at one time or another, confront others with disagreements or misunderstandings. There are never shortages of topics or situations that will prompt difficult conversations.

DIFFICULT CONVERSATIONS

Difficult conversations can be about anything that may arouse conflict or disagreements. They can also be about things that may be embarrassing, such as asking for a raise or complaining to a neighbor about their barking dog. People are usually reluctant to open a difficult conversation out of fear of the consequences. Ironically, those people who do open a difficult conversation usually feel better after discussing the issues.

According to the book *Difficult Conversations: How to Discuss What Matters Most*, by Douglas Stone, Bruce Patton, and Sheila Heen,[1] underlying every difficult conversation are three deeper conversations. The "what happened?" conversation usually involves disagreement over what happened, what should happen, and who is to blame. The "feelings" conversation is about people's emotions and their authenticity. The "identity" conversation is an internal conversation that each party has with herself, over what the situation tells her about who she is.

The authors identify common errors that people make in these sorts of conversations. The key to having effective, productive conversations is to recognize the presence of these deeper conversations, to avoid the common errors, and to turn difficult conversations into learning conversations.

The "what happened?" conversation

The first mistake that people make as they consider what happened is that they assume they are looking at a factual matter and that their view of the matter is right. Although the parties might agree on the basic facts, they may differ in their interpretations of what the facts mean and of what is important. To move toward a learning conversation, parties must shift from certainty about their own views to curiosity about the other's views of the situation.

The second mistake comes from misunderstanding the parties' intentions. People tend to assume that they know what the other's intentions are. However, our own beliefs about another's intentions are often wrong. We base our assumptions on our own feelings; if I feel hurt, then you must have meant to be hurtful. We also think the worst of others and the best of ourselves. Remain open-minded about your own interpretation of their intent. Avoid this mistake by acknowledging the other's feelings and by considering the possibility of your own complex motives.

A third mistake in the "what happened?" conversation occurs when parties focus on assigning blame. "Focusing on blame is a bad idea, because it inhibits our ability to learn what's really causing the problem and to do anything meaningful to correct it."[2] The solution is to focus on mapping each party's contribution to the situation. The contribution should emphasize understanding causes, joint responsibility, and avoiding future problems. Acknowledging one's own contributions can help shift the other party away from blaming.

The "feelings" conversation

Difficult conversations are difficult because there are feelings involved. Expressing emotions is difficult. Many people frame difficult conversations in ways that ignore their emotional content. Unexpressed feelings can leak back into the conversation and can preoccupy people so that they are unable to be good listeners. The solution is for the parties to identify and understand their feelings, negotiate them, and share them clearly.

The first step in expressing feelings is to acknowledge that they are an important part of the situation, whether they are "rational" or not. Parties should convey the full range and complexity of their feelings, and they should avoid rushing to evaluate the feelings expressed. To be effective in sharing requires that the parties acknowledge each other's feelings.

The "identity" conversation

Some conversations are difficult because they threaten or challenge a person's sense of who they are. Managing the internal identity conversation requires learning which issues are most important to each person's identity and learning how to adapt your identity in healthy ways. The book *Difficult Conversations* notes that the more easily you can admit to your own mistakes, your own mixed intentions, and your own contributions to the problem, the more balanced you will feel during the conversation and the higher the chances it will go well. Other ways to maintain a balanced sense of self in difficult conversations include not trying to control the other's reactions, instead preparing for their reaction, imagining yourself in the future, or just taking a break from the conversation.

HOW TO DEAL WITH DIFFICULT CONVERSATIONS

So what can you do to make these conversations less difficult?

Let it go

Sometimes difficult issues should be raised, but sometimes it is best to let them go. There is no simple rule for deciding which is which, but in *Difficult Conversations*, the authors do suggest some things to consider in making such decisions. Working through the three conversations on your own will give a clearer understanding of the situation, and so a better basis for deciding. Some apparent conflicts between people turn out to mainly conflict within one person, such as an identity crisis.

If you decide not to raise the issue, these four attitudes may help you let go. First, you are not responsible for fixing the situation; the most you can do is your best. Second, remind yourself that the other party has limitations too. Third, separate the issue from your identity. Fourth, recognize that you can let go and still care about the issue.

If you can't let it go

Most conversations fail because people begin by describing the problem from their own perspective, which implies a judgment about the other person and provokes a defensive response. Instead, start conversations from the perspective of a third party that describes (or at least acknowledges) the difference between the parties' views in neutral terms. The opening should then invite the other party to join in a conversation, seeking mutual understanding or joint problem-solving.

Listening is a crucially important part of handling difficult conversations. It helps us understand the other person, and the feeling of having been heard makes the other more able to listen themselves. The key to being a good listener is to be truly curious and concerned about the other person. Techniques that can help show that you care and are concerned include asking open questions, asking for more concrete information, asking questions that explore the three conversations, and giving the other the option of not answering. Avoid questions that are statements. Do not cross-examine the other person. Paraphrasing them helps clarify and check your own understanding. Acknowledge the power and importance of the other person's feelings, both expressed and unexpressed. Often, simply raising or clarifying an issue after listening is enough to resolve the difficulty.

The single most important rule about managing the interaction is this: You can't move the conversation in a more positive direction until the other person feels heard and understood. When in doubt about how to proceed, listen.

We often find every excuse to avoid these talks. Don't do this! You need to nip what bothers you in the bud and do it as early as possible. Confrontation becomes more difficult as the delay increases. The problem then continues to fester, and bad feelings build up until it just percolates and boils over.

There is probably an art to having difficult conversations, and there are many books written on the subject. One of the most important points is that you don't let it simmer. Make sure you go into it with the attitude that there are always two sides to a story, and somewhere in the middle lies the truth. Also, don't do all the talking. Listening is difficult, but it is immensely important that you do this. There may be new information that you were not aware of, and it may change the entire dynamic of your perspective. The bottom line is to keep an open mind to any controversy. Don't let the infection set in!

Food for thought

Leadership should not avoid difficult conversations. Problems, disagreements, and bad feelings should be addressed quickly and not wait until later or tomorrow. Always listen with intent and keep an open mind.

CHAPTER 27

DON'T FALL FOR THE MOMMY AND DADDY GAMES

"There are two sides to a story, and
somewhere in the middle is the truth."

—**Anonymous**

A common interaction at home is the mom-dad-kid triad. The kid wants something or wants to go somewhere. The mom says, "No, not until you clean your room!" The kid then goes to the dad. He says, "Sure!" This effectively weakens the parental controls and strengthens the child's manipulative abilities. As most of us have experienced, this same scenario occurs at the workplace, especially where there are inadequate communication processes between the leaders themselves and a weak organizational reporting structure.

People often want to gain the most by putting out the least amount of effort. This is not to say that all people are this way, but it is a characteristic that I have witnessed and dealt with for years. Once, a front desk clerk declared to a coworker, "I'll start working harder once they give me a raise!"

Several years ago, I hired three dentists at the same time. They had all been friends during their post–dental school training, and I even interviewed them together. They had great chemistry, and I reasoned that they probably would work very well together—efficiently and productively.

This turned out to be a big mistake. We referred to them as the Three Amigos—not in a fond way, but more out of frustration with the way they constantly manipulated everyone for their personal gain. They certainly had chemistry—the way gangs have chemistry when they rob banks or are involved in white-collar heists. They constantly challenged our policies and protocols to find shortcuts or to get extra benefits for themselves. Once, the COO caught them manipulating the patient-scheduling guidelines in order to get extra time off for themselves. A major conflict ensued between these "bad guys" and the COO, who was a stickler for accountability and following the rules.

The Three Amigos' strategy, unbeknownst to me at the time, was to bypass the COO and come to me about issues with logic and information that were not always true. I found myself agreeing with some of their reasoning and approved certain projects or schemes that the COO had already denied. This created a significant rift between me and the COO, as I was effectively usurping her authority. It was clear our management team was weak, and we were easily manipulated. Like in the movie *Cool Hand Luke*, "what we have here is a failure to communicate."

Eventually, the COO and other members of my team worked out a solution centered on the principles of the concept of the chain of command. First, we had failed very badly to communicate among our management team, and we agreed that our first priority was to correct this issue. Next, we agreed, at all levels of management, to always use the chain of command when it came to decision-making responsibilities. Third, we also agreed that I (the CEO) would not override my management team's decisions and authority when presented with information by anyone outside the team. By avoiding this, I would avoid weakening their authority and rendering them ineffective. Finally, if a seemingly controversial issue arose, and we did not have a chance to speak to any of the leadership team, then decisions would be deferred back to the relevant employee's supervisor. This would keep everyone on track for decisions and actions and would mitigate severe conflicts among the management team. After realizing that we had stopped their mommy and daddy games, the Three Amigos soon resigned.

Food for thought

People will often try to manipulate leaders for their own personal gain. You can put an end to that practice with solid policies, protocols, and excellent communication processes between the leadership team. This will prevent the mommy and daddy games so prevalent among kids!

CHAPTER 28

DON'T FEAR FEAR

"The only thing we have to fear is fear itself."

—Franklin Delano Roosevelt

Fear surrounds us. Most of it is perpetrated by others, but some is self-imposed, birthed by our own imagination or perceptions. Fear is often used to control others for good and bad purposes. Some religions use it to help instill good behavior—the so-called fear-of-God phenomenon. Politicians use fear to get their way—votes, money, and power: "If you don't vote for me, you will live in dire poverty and probably die very young." Authoritarian figures such as company bosses, drill sergeants, or even educators use it to bring out the best of their direct reports, soldiers, and students.

Self-imposed fear can be so overpowering that people may become dysfunctional. People with dementia, schizophrenia, and neurosis may suffer from hallucinations and paranoid delusions resulting in debilitating behavior.

However, self-imposed fear without the associated neuropsychological precursors can have positive effects. For example, some may use fear as a self-awareness tool and overcome obstacles by, perhaps, going the extra mile to compensate for their weakness that led to the fear. Consider the following story as an illustration of overcoming fear through awareness and compensation. (Compensation in this example refers to the psychology definition where an individual attempts to make up for some real or imagined deficiency of personality or behavior by developing or stressing another aspect of the personality when substituting a different form of behavior.)

"What's holding you back?" my dad asked.

He had discovered that I planned to quit my high school's freshman cross-country team after finishing nearly last place in my first competitive race. My head hung down as long, hippie-length hair effectively covered my face. I didn't want to look at my dad, and I didn't want him to see my face. I felt so ashamed and humiliated for being such a dud competitor. It particularly hurt when people laughed at me as I barely crossed the finish line on skinny, wobbly legs. I know he sensed that I was afraid to run another race.

Dad had recently retired from the US Army and now worked as a mailman. He was a combat veteran of two military engagements—World War II and the Korean conflict—so he knew a thing or two about the worst kinds of fear. He also knew that to overcome fear, we needed to confront it through self-confidence and belief.

He repeated his question, this time in a firmer voice: "What's holding you back to get out there and try to do better the next time?" After my silence, he said, "Look, I don't expect you to win, but I expect you to face your fear of losing. When you fall, you need to stand back up and walk. When you get tired of walking, you run. Then make sure you run hard, until you get there. Don't be afraid to fail or look bad. Learn from it, and always believe in yourself."

I listened. Dad took off early from work and showed up at my next race. Even though I was at the back of the pack, he rushed onto the course and yelled words of encouragement as I ran by. His faith in me helped shed fears and encouraged confidence. As a result, I ended up with a great high school experience enjoying both athletic and academic successes, all because my dad believed in me.

Now, as a senior citizen, I look back at my lifetime full of numerous physical activities, travel, and adventures and understand how my dad taught me to battle and win over my fears through encouragement, perseverance, and belief in myself. A nasty fall, recently, on Mt. Elbrus, in Russia, prevented me from reaching the summit. Immediately, that night in our tent, my climbing partner and daughter Abbey and I made plans to return the following year to try again. No fears! I learned how to deal with it, and I am no longer afraid to fail when so much can be gained by simply trying and having confidence.

What holds you back? For many people, it is fear. We fear making the wrong decisions. We fear rejection. We fear failure. We fear loss. The list is endless, and all of it can be overcome.

WHAT IS FEAR?

Fear is nature's neurophysiological alarm system. It warns us of approaching threats. We have all experienced fear. Sometimes, it is even a little bit fun to get scared. For example, many of us like roller coasters, visiting haunted houses during Halloween, and watching horror movies.

The Twilight Zone episode "The Monsters Are Due on Maple Street" aired on March 4, 1960. The opening scene is akin to an idyllic Norman Rockwell–like portrayal of a late summer afternoon on Maple Street, USA. Kids eagerly run toward an ice cream cart to dig into their refreshing treats; dads wash and tinker with their cars; a mom comes outside with her apron on, presumably preparing for dinner.

This serenity is suddenly interrupted by a strange rippling sound accompanied by flashes of light overhead. People stop and peer up at the sky and immediately conclude that it was a meteor that intruded on the afternoon activities. The disturbance is soon dismissed, and people resume their activities.

But strange things begin to happen. Cars and lawnmowers do not start. The electrical power to appliances, lights, telephones, and even power tools also stops working. People become concerned when a neighborhood child, by the name of Tommy, tells the street neighbors that he read a story of an alien invasion where the aliens appear human-like and live as if they belong in the neighborhood. He believed this was why everything stopped working. There must be aliens among us—scouts who were preparing for an invasion of Earth.

At first, the neighborhood crowd was dismissive of the rubbish talk, but people quickly became paranoid and suspicious of everyone around them. Friends and neighbors were now suspected of being aliens in disguise. Squabbling and hysteria ensued, fights broke out, and a man was shot and killed. It eventually led to a riot.

The camera gently pans toward the horizon and takes us to another scene, where two figures standing next to a flying saucer are watching the chaos of Maple Street. They are holding on to an alien gadget that is manipulating the neighborhood's power source. They discuss how easy it would be to conquer Earth just by disrupting the typical pattern of life, prompting paranoia, panic, and fear.

Because of its powerful nature, fear is commonly used for benevolent and malicious purposes. Warning others about consequences is typically a good use of fear. However, despite your good intentions, it may unintentionally result in bad outcomes. In Tommy's case, he wanted to warn the residents of Maple Street, so he told them a story without factual confirmation. Making fearful statements without facts is a dangerous use of fear.

Fear is often rooted in the unknown and anticipation. For example, many of us feared the dark when we were kids, and some still do. When darkness falls on us, our sight diminishes, and suddenly, the environment becomes an unknown. Our imagination then runs rampant, resulting in anxiety and worry. This may result in irrational behavior, much like that of the residents of Maple Street.

The evolutionary advantage of anxiety is that worrying about danger forces people to take fewer risks, seek safety, and focus on doing things well.[1] The protective part of this cascade is that our senses become sharper, our thinking is quicker, and the fight-or-flight response kicks into full gear.[2] From an evolutionary point of view, those who could react quickly survived and reproduced, assuring the continuation of the species; that fight-or-flight instinct was beneficial and innate, but it can now be a hindrance.

The Twilight Zone episode illustrates how powerful fear is. Leaders are fearful of the effects of their decisions and must choose how to wield fear to control others for positive or negative purposes. Will you use it for good or evil purposes?

HOW FEAR AFFECTS LEADERS

Fear is a part of all leaders' work life. It can play an even greater role as a tool to control others. I have found that many leaders have at least three work-related fears associated with their role: making decisions, taking chances, and doing unconventional things. It's also common in everyday people doing everyday things. For example, when I wanted to quit cross-country, I was afraid to take a chance with another sport, not wanting to be humiliated again. I was too worried about what people would think about me and never thought of how I could improve my running abilities until my dad talked with me. Fear had simply frozen me.

Leaders often fear making decisions

"Did I make the right decision?" is a fear many leaders have. "Will my decision hurt anyone, or will someone lose their job because of what I did?" Many decisions a leader makes are based on intuition and analytical data. Analytics, however, may not always be accurate or useful when making decisions about people; it does not take the human factor into play. For example, accountants are good at making decisions based on raw financial data, such as direct revenue and direct expenses. However, they are not as good (a generalization, of course) at the indirect benefits a cost may have for the company that may have nothing to do with direct revenue. The process of deciding becomes a taxing experience when fear gets in the way. If a decision is wrong, then it can hurt people, cause job loss, and disrupt families. The company could be hurt to the point of failure. Some leaders fear making decisions so much that they are consumed with the possibility of making the wrong decision, and they end up not making any.

An important parental decision is whether to vaccinate your children or not. Many parents are fearful of the potential side effects their child might suffer, so they decide not to; however, the medical literature indicates a very high safety rate and clear benefits of vaccination, the primary one being that deadly infectious diseases are prevented.[3] However, adverse vaccine side effects are also always a possibility, no matter how many safeguards are put in place. There are no drugs or vaccines that I know about that do not have any side effects.

Although this is a simplistic example, it demonstrates that people may have deficiencies even with simple decisions that may affect others. But doing nothing is also a choice.

Leaders fear taking chances

After 35 years of leading my health clinics, I was in the position of developing another health access point for patients who might have difficulty accessing health care. I purchased a building from the city of Youngstown, in a food desert. This is a sociological term for residential areas with little or poor access to fresh produce and other healthy items. There may be no supermarkets in the area, or they may not be well stocked. Convenience stores and quick shops, however, are often prevalent in low-income areas. They carry the good-tasting, high-sugar, and salty foods, but those foods are very addictive and bad for your health. This new location was also in a high-crime area, so people did not spend time running or walking in the neighborhood. There are no safe playgrounds, basketball courts, or parks in the area, so the residents rarely get enough exercise.

The lack of exercise and a poor diet are the perfect recipe for obesity. Medically, we know that obesity is the leading cause of chronic diseases such as diabetes, cardiovascular diseases, even cancers and mental health conditions.[4] I wanted to open a health facility that addressed these social determinants. I envisioned having greenhouses, walking trails, community kitchens, and exercise areas on this property. I even wanted to have a working merry-go-round carousel for the kids.

I got a lot of questions and even pushback with this idea. How do we make money on something like this? We are increasing our liability by having walking and exercise events. What if the kitchen catches on fire? What if kids fall off the carousel horses? The skeptics went on and on. Most younger leaders would be afraid to do something outside the box, but I believe this is where the separation of good leaders and great leaders happens. Leaders cannot be afraid to take chances.

Good leaders should not get handcuffed by indecisions due to fear. If leaders do the right things for the right reasons and do them the right way, the fear will dissipate, and we move forward.

In the previous scenario, I knew, through dealing with health-care polices over the years, that the health-care delivery programs and reimbursement policies are an ever-changing paradigm. The most current reimbursement models are described as value-based structures, while historically these models were volume-driven. This means that health-care practitioners in the past were paid on productivity. The more patients they saw, the more they could bill for. The value-based program is based on health outcomes—how well our patients are doing and not by how many patients are seen. The holistic health-care delivery model I envision addresses the body as a whole, along with the social conditions the individual lives under—the social determinants that affect health. Believing this is the best model for future delivery of health care, I have planned to move forward with this project; however, sadly with the onset of the COVID-19 pandemic, the project is now temporarily on hold. Architectural plans and partial financing have been established, so this project will be on its way soon!

Leaders fear thinking and doing things that are unconventional

People are generally afraid to get out of their comfort zone and to do things differently. They may say, "If that's the way it's always been done, then that's the way we should always continue to do it." But there is always more than one way to do just about anything. In medicine, there are usually many ways to handle different types of diseases. Some work, and some don't, depending on innumerable factors, but we have multiple options to try. Leaders need to stick their neck out sometimes and just go with it.

LEADERS USING FEAR TO CONTROL

The use of fear to control people can have both positive and negative results. For example, consider the Christmas song "Santa Claus Is Coming to Town." Get past the great melody, and with further examination, it suggests threats, spying on children, and intimidation. Be good or else—and don't you dare cry! Children who are not good will be punished by not getting toys. Adults often use this tactic to elicit better behavior from children. The positive aspect is that children will probably behave better and parents are glad to give their kids presents.

As a physician, I have frequently witnessed this parental tactic when examining a squirmy and crying child. Mothers frequently yelled at their kids, "If you're not good, I'm not getting you McDonald's, and you can't go to the playground!" Or "If you're not good, that doctor is going to give you a shot!" The kids usually got shots anyway, but they behaved well enough to get a good medical exam and get their vaccines.

As a leader, you must consider very carefully whether using fear to control your employees is an effective means of leadership.

The negative effects of fear

In the previously discussed *Twilight Zone* episode, we see the aliens use fear to produce negative behavior in the townsfolk, resulting in division and distrust. It is a positive effect for the aliens, because it caused chaos and weakness among the human beings; however, it was certainly a negative effect for the earthlings.

We often see leaders use fear to control people for political reasons. During the late 1960s and early 1970s, the war in Vietnam continued to escalate. The political leaders at the time told us that if we did not stop the Communists dead in their tracks now, there would be a domino effect of socialism that would overtake the world. Country after country would eventually fall to the scourge of Communism, one by one. "This is a threat to our very existence," they said. "We must stop this spread now, and we need to be prepared to die for our freedom." Our leaders used fear to control us. We continue to see this every day in the news now, especially in politics. With mass media, the fear tactics have gotten even stronger.

When leaders predominantly use fear as a tool to get people to do things and to frequently control others, they attain negative results. Positive teamwork is undermined. People cannot do their jobs effectively if they are too consumed with gossip and discussing how bad working for the boss has become. Fear often creates workplace cliques that prevent people from speaking up. As a result, the goals of the organization often become an afterthought.

Employees working under a leader who uses fear to control their direct report staff are often concerned about potential consequences or repercussions if they voice their fear, such as being laughed at or not taken seriously. They also fear being labeled as weak, which may affect their promotion opportunities.

Fear may also affect work attendance. A 2005 study from the US Department of Labor estimated that 3 percent of an employer's workforce is absent on a given day, representing a cost between 20.9 percent and 22.1 percent of total payroll. Sickness and depression occur much more in difficult work environments, and they can lead to absenteeism. Interestingly, in a 2000 study by the Bureau of Labor, a heavy workload had no effect on depression; it was the work environment itself and the feeling of being treated unfairly by the management that had the greatest effects on employees' moods.[5]

The positive effects of fear

In the military, green recruits are subjected to fear almost immediately. They are bullied, yelled at, and screamed at from the very beginning without provocation. Soldiers stay in line because they don't want this fear to be imposed on them. In this case, fear is demonstrated first as a warning to avoid future bad behavior. It is preventive and will possibly save lives in future combat situations. In the civilian world, fear typically comes after an infraction occurs. It is then a consequence, but the positive is that the employee will learn after the fact and possibly avoid the unpleasant situation again.

Consider why employees follow rules. In many cases, entry-level employees do so because they want to keep their jobs, get paid, and maybe even get a promotion. Fear of consequences or of endangering advancement makes them follow rules. Again, this is a positive effect of fear: Order is established.

Religions, schools, and prisons are other examples of using fear to gain a certain desirable behavior. In many religions, if you are not good, then you risk spending eternity in hell. When I was in school, if we were caught talking in class, we had to draw a circle on the chalkboard and put our nose in the circle. It was humiliating, and breathing the chalk dust probably made us sick, but we avoided talking in class after that so that we could listen and learn. Prisons put you in solitary confinement—or worse—if you misbehave. This sort of behavioral control through fear may avoid future fights, injuries, and even deaths.

Fear is not always a bad thing. Recall that fear is often a reactionary emotion to failure, adversity, mistakes, and enemies (FAME) that can elicit anxiety and worry. This may lead to irrational responses, or you could turn it around into a positive like the following story.

My mom was lonely, afraid, and unhappy when we first moved to the United States. Not being able to speak the language fluently and prejudice against Japanese people made her sad and unsettled her. She frequently threatened to go back to Japan when my parents fought. As a six-year-old who had known my mom as the only caretaker for all my life, I was terrified. The yelling was frightening, but her threats were even more alarming.

To compensate for that fear, I overcompensated by becoming a high achiever and maybe a little bit of a control freak. I wanted to make sure that I was always smart enough to control events and people who could instill a fear in me. Not until much later in life did I realize I had been successful to make my mom proud of me so that she would not leave. Fear forced me to work hard.

It is ironic how some fear, which is depicted as a negative emotion, can be used to elicit a consequence of good. Leaders should use fear to make the best of a situation and should use it to teach and improve their staff's working habits.

Food for thought

Leaders should understand the power of fear and should use it to help keep order and encourage others to learn and overcome the negativity it has on people. Think of how fear has either motivated you to do something for the better or prevented you from acting. Did fear help or hold you back when it came to accomplishing something good and worthwhile? Is fear holding you back?

CHAPTER 29

DON'T RUN OVER THE CAT

"An ounce of prevention is
worth a pound of cure."
—Benjamin Franklin

Kitty was an outside cat. He had a gray coat with splotches of white, and a small white star adorned his forehead. He came to live with us when he was about six months old. Not long after, he slipped out of my 14-year-old daughter's arms and rapidly escaped into the woods. Teary-eyed, Sarah was devastated. She had wanted a cat for so long, and after only a few days, he ran away!

We called off the search after two days of combing through the woods and nearby neighborhoods. He had vanished without a trace.

A week later, out of nowhere and without fanfare, Kitty suddenly reappeared. He sauntered slowly from the woods, as if tired, and plopped himself onto the back porch. In a sitting position, he began wiping his face with his licked paws as if he had not a care in the world. From that day on, he became an outside cat, and we knew he would always make his way back home.

Around the age of 15, Kitty began to venture out less until he permanently stayed in the garage. It was heated, and we had a nice sleeping area for him. A problem with this arrangement was that when we drove our cars into the garage, it was difficult to track his whereabouts. We all sensed that it was inevitable that an accident would occur one day, but we took no precautions to prevent this. I don't know why.

So it was. One day Kitty got hit in the garage, leaving his left front leg bone broken. By now, he was too old to make a reasonable recovery and might not have even been able to make it past the anesthesia. The veterinarian compassionately recommended euthanasia.

POOR PREVENTION PRACTICES

Kitty's tale is a horrible story where we failed to practice prevention. Although I was aware that this was bound to happen to poor Kitty, I did nothing to prevent it. Shame on me!

There are so many illustrations of how valuable the practice of prevention is, but unfortunately, there are an equal number of examples of how often we avoid it—human nature, I suppose. We eat poorly selected foods—too much and too often. We drink too much alcohol, don't get enough exercise, don't sleep enough, or sleep too much. We spend way too much time in front of screens—computer, television, and movie—and munch on tasty but unhealthy snacks. All these choices take a toll on our lives and result in shortened life spans and poor health.

If we took care of ourselves, many chronic diseases could be avoided. We could enjoy wonderful and healthy lives while saving society a bundle of money that could be used to improve other qualities of life or to help individuals struggling with diseases that aren't preventable.

Another important life matter that we don't plan well for is death. We, of course, cannot prevent death, but we can plan a better end-of-life experience for our loved ones and prevent future family discord. Arranging a will, appointing a durable power of attorney, and selecting a health-care proxy will save much grief for everyone. Without these documents, government entities will take over all aspects of your life. Beneficiaries will battle one another; your wealth may be divided and stolen, not according to your wishes but those of others. We can prevent a lot of heartaches for our loved ones by doing some simple proactive prevention.

LEADERSHIP AND PREVENTION

Leaders are in an outstanding position to take the lead in prevention practices. As a pediatrician, I often taught my patients' parents the concept of anticipatory guidance—an excellent set of preventive measures designed to keep kids safe by addressing such topics as firearm safety and sexual activity counseling in adolescents. For parents of toddlers, we advocated plugging up power outlets, putting locks on cabinets where toxic cleaning materials are stored, and setting up gates by the staircases for the little ones.

Most leaders know there are business advantages to practicing prevention. Policies, employee training programs, continuing education, and human resource monitoring are designed as preventive components for any organized business group. Consider the Occupational Safety and Health Administration (OSHA) as an example of prevention practice policies. Contrary to some beliefs, OSHA is designed as a valuable tool to help businesses prevent injuries or death at the workplace, saving businesses future liability costs, as well as protecting their most valuable resource—the employee.

In 2009, OSHA reviewed the illness and injury prevention programs in 231 companies with 100 or more employees. Eight states either provided incentives or required a program that resulted in a decrease in injuries and incidences from 60 percent to 9 percent.[1]

Texas had a program under its workers' compensation commission from 1991 to 2005 that identified the most hazardous workplaces. Those employers were required to develop and implement injury and illness prevention programs. The reduction in injuries, over a four-year period (1992–1995), averaged 63 percent each year.[2] No doubt, this saved the company many hours of productivity, as well as improved personal quality of lives for the employees.

Alcoa, during a period when then CEO Paul O'Neill, a recognized safety visionary and leader, was in charge, began focusing on becoming the world's safest company with a goal of zero harm. Their annual earnings went from $0.20 per share in 1994 to $1.41 in 1999. Their sales grew an average of 15 percent per year during the same period. By 2000, it was 5 times safer to work at Alcoa than it had been 10 years earlier.[3]

Companies and organizations should be strong advocates for employees' health by encouraging healthy daily activities. I began an organizational wellness program a few years ago that included competitions, program completions, and other activities to entice people to participate. We provide flavored carbonated water dispensers and healthy-snack vending machines for our staff. In just a couple of years, over 1,589 pounds of weight were lost by 90 employees, 77 participated in 87,815 minutes of strength training, 247,646,626 steps were taken by 166 different employees, and 1,345 miles were run by 24 different employees.[4] Consider the possibilities of some of our employees' health status if we had not done this program. Leadership focused on emphasizing prevention, which may have saved lives and most certainly improved lives for members of my company.

Leaders can and should practice preventive measures to not only prevent employees' injury or illness that will affect their ability to work but also help them remain financially stable and maintain their livelihood. Certainly, the toll of an illness or injury on not just the victim but their coworkers, families, and communities as well can be devastating.

The bottom line is that we do not have to run over the cat. If only I had taken preventive action, Kitty might have avoided an untimely death. Rest in peace, Kitty!

Food for thought

Leaders should always practice preventive measures in both personal and professional lives. Has anything happened to you like it did to me with Kitty's story? Something you could have prevented if only you had paid more attention and taken action sooner?

CHAPTER 30

DON'T DRAIN THE EMOTIONAL BANK ACCOUNT

"Emotions are the language of the soul."

—Karla McLaren, American writer

Emotional intelligence, sometimes referred to as emotional leadership or emotional quotient, was first described in a 1964 article titled "The Communication of Emotional Meaning."[1] The concept refers to an ability to have insight into others' emotions, as well as your own. Having the ability to read signals through body language, facial gestures, and verbal cues, and to then react to them appropriately, are important requirements for success.

Most literature discusses five primary characteristics of emotional intelligence.

FIVE TYPES OF EMOTIONAL INTELLIGENCE

Self-awareness

Self-awareness is a person's ability to have insight into themselves. How well do you know yourself, and how well can you reflect on your actions and statements? For example, if you are upset with someone and perhaps used ill language, do you have the ability and self-awareness to later realize that was not right and to apologize and make amends? Do you ever look in the mirror and reflect on the day?

Self-regulation

How well do you control your behavior? Can you maintain calmness and avoid reacting badly to a bad situation? Are you able to take a deep breath before you respond?

Empathy

Do you have the ability to recognize others' feelings and act positively on it? Can you envision yourself in someone else's shoes? Are you able to comfort them or deeply listen to their troubles and understand why they feel poorly or sad?

Social skills

Social skills are your ability to work with others. Do you possess people and interpersonal skills to work together with others or to get a group together to accomplish something? Are you capable of talking with others, not above them?

Motivation

Are you able to get things done? Are you a go-getter, a doer? Will you work hard to get things accomplished?

After many years of leadership, I have come to value the concept of high emotional intelligence as a critical attribute for good leadership. Being able to read people through a sixth sense, by intuition and insight, or to interpret body language is a huge advantage for leaders. People appreciate that you can understand their needs. Your emotional quotient functions as a type of feedback of your own emotions and allows adjustments in how you act, what you say, and what you do through your interactions with others. This is how we build respect, trust, confidence, and belief in our ability to lead.

MR. FITZ

The following true story is a great example of how *not* to be a leader. It is a great illustration of lacking emotional intelligence.

During the last few days of August 1969, I became a freshman at a rural high school near a large military base. The student body was made up of an eclectic mixture of local farm kids and military brats holding travel resumes that put touring rock stars to shame.

There were poor kids and rich ones, including kids like me, who looked Asian but had Anglicized names because their military dads had married Japanese, Korean, or Chinese women. My classmates were from India, Africa, and the South Pacific. A few Australians and South Americans peppered our classrooms too. The potpourri of personalities was sometimes overwhelming for a small Kentucky high school to handle.

The wide diversity of students and teachers brought about an atmosphere of helter-skelter that, for some unknown reason, begat a small minority of teachers who were dysfunctional and cruel. Mr. Fitz was one teacher who became our tormentor during the entire ninth-grade experience.

I first met him in my third-period health and phys ed class—an all-boys group with a lot of raw adolescent humor rooted in a bed of stupidity. This is where I learned about human ugliness, abuse, and just plain meanness.

Mr. Fitz was a true martinet. He drilled, yelled, punched, and made us stand at attention at the beginning of every class while he called roll. Once, a boy named Hoefer (we were always referred to by our last names) didn't say "here" loud enough, and Fitz, without uttering a sound, grabbed him by the back of the neck and simultaneously kicked him behind the knees. This caused him to buckle and fall hard, banging his head on the way down. Fitz then dragged poor Hoefer up by the neck and dragged him across the gym floor and into his office.

Ten minutes later, frozen with fear and still standing motionlessly at attention, we watched Fitz and Hoefer emerge from behind closed doors. With a noticeable limp and slumped posture, a bloody nose, and a goose egg on the left side of his head, the boy followed close behind Fitz as they made their way back to the line. Hoefer resumed his place and promptly yelled in a high-pitched, screeching voice, "Here!"

Another student, Jackson, was short, skinny, and hyper. One time, he impulsively climbed the gym bleachers to the top, where he jumped onto a trampoline that Fitz had set up for the next class. We were horrified at the spectacle as Jackson, propelled by gravity, hurtled toward the trampoline. One bounce later, he was on the gym floor, writhing in pain. Mr. Fitz was laughing and kept yelling at the boy to stop being a "turd" and to get up, even kicking him on the rear end to entice him. The next day, Jackson was wearing a cast on his left arm—the result of a compound fracture.

Our health classes, held every other day alternating with the phys ed sessions, were no better. Mr. Fitz swore he would never give us any pop quizzes, but he sprang one on us just about every week. If we couldn't answer questions in class, he made us get on our toes and elbows (these days, they call it planks) for the remainder of the class. If we couldn't hold the stance, he'd smack our behinds with a paddle that had holes drilled into it to inflict sharper pain to our bottoms.

Once, on an exam, he said he was going to be nice by giving us a clue about the bonus question: Who's buried at Grant's Tomb? He warned us that we better not put "Grant" as the answer or he'd flunk us all. I put down "general and later president Ulysses S. Grant." Turns out, I was the only kid who used the forbidden name, but I was the only one who got the question right. He told us that he was trying to trick us and wanted the answer I had put down. It was not just the name Grant; he wanted his full name and description. I didn't have to get on my toes and elbows that day!

Mr. Fitz was disorganized, duplicitous, mean, and consistently not a nice man. He lied, never did what he said he would do, and constantly played mind games with our adolescence. When we were done with him and went on to be sophomores, we never looked back. We never knew what happened to him, nor did anyone care. Mr. Fitz sorely lacked emotional intelligence.

THE EMOTIONAL BANK ACCOUNT

The emotional bank account is a mental tool and works exactly like a passbook savings account. I first read about this concept in a Stephen Covey book titled *7 Habits of Highly Effective People*. You deposit good deeds into this account by doing things you say you are going to do or are expected to do, such as promptly answering your emails, telephone calls, or letters. For example, most people are communicating with you for a reason, and they expect or anticipate a timely reply. When you don't reply, you essentially withdraw on this account. The account represents trust, timeliness, good faith, and confidence by others toward you as a leader.

Another example of draining the emotional bank account is the characteristic of people never admitting to doing something wrong. It is always someone else's fault. There are many who blame others for their troubles and very rarely take responsibility.

When you write a birthday card to someone or send a message of thanks and a "good job" comment, you are making deposits. Patting your employees on the back and giving them praises have the same effect. Smiling and saying hi genuinely, as if you are truly glad to see them, are other deposits. Even small talk with someone you don't know but are deeply listening to constitutes a deposit.

Several years ago, an attorney from out of town asked for a business meeting with me. My time being so limited and me not having information from or about him, I reluctantly agreed to meet. When I walked into the conference room for the meeting, he had already been seated across the large table. He immediately rose, walked around the table to shake my hand, smiled pleasantly, looked directly in my eyes, and said, "I am so honored to meet you, Dr. Dwinnells!" How cordial. I instantly liked this man, and we ended up having a great business meeting about an idea he had. He made a deposit into his emotional bank account, and I stayed engaged during our meeting and his presentation.

It is clear that the bank account concept works both ways. I want to do good and help those who have a great emotional bank account, because when I engage with them, I reciprocate their good behavior and manners. I then make deposits too. But when I deal with people who are negative in their accounts—for instance, they are reading their cell phone texts while I'm talking to them—it makes me upset, and I say something negative and out of character for me. This effectively withdraws from both of our emotional bank accounts.

A good case study about emotional bank accounts is an exchange many of us witnessed on the evening news involving then presidential candidate Joe Biden. He became angry when a Detroit factory worker provoked him about Second Amendment rights. Although the former vice president's response was understandable, it made him appear less presidential, perhaps causing a "withdrawal" from his emotional bank account.[2]

Emotional bank accounts build up over time. When things happen and you need your workers' support, you will always get it if you have currency in it. However, if you are like Mr. Fitz, you will end up with an emotional bank account consistently drained or in the negative.

Food for thought

Keep a mental log of your emotional bank account. At the end of the day, tally up your deposits and withdrawals. Perhaps this will give you a balance of how your day progressed. Try to keep a positive balance in your account!

CHAPTER 31

DON'T TAKE GOSSIP AS GOSPEL

"Great minds discuss ideas; average minds discuss events; small minds discuss people."

—Eleanor Roosevelt

Communication is the key to a more productive, efficient, and effective organization; closer family interactions and understanding; and more fulfilling relationships. The core components of the receptive portion of communication are our five senses: listening, seeing, touching, and even tasting and smelling. As a physician, I have routinely used all five receptors to help me diagnose and manage patient illnesses. Yes, even taste: Patients, especially kids, often ask, "Does the medicine taste bad?" and I know the answer because I've sampled most of them during my lifetime.

Expression or transmission of communication happens through natural human tools, such as speaking or hand, facial, and body gestures, and through artificial human means of audio and visual broadcasting with electronic gadgets, such as computers, radios, and television. Despite these wondrous and marvelous abilities to communicate, a significant flaw exists in the accuracy of information, events, people, and ideas. We often don't know whether we can trust these devices or even our own senses to tell us the truth. Other people are an even less reliable source of true information. We always wonder, "Is it gossip or truly gospel?"

GOSPEL

When I receive information, I would like it to be as close to gospel as possible. I always ask, "How do you know this?" or "What proof do you have to confirm your conclusions?" or "Where did you get this information?" As a leader, I depend on accurate and objective information to be able to make good decisions. Information without truth or substantiated as the truth is merely gossip and can be dangerous if it is wholly believed and if actions and reactions are undertaken.

GOSSIP

"If they aren't true, why do you care?"

I ask this question whenever an employee complains about what so-and-so said about them. Many people are often deeply affected by what others say about them, even if it isn't the truth. I'm confused about why these people who are talked about and who know it isn't true get upset about it anyway. We see this phenomenon on social media, and it occasionally leads to suicide or murder because of intense verbal bullying leading to deep emotional despondency.

Workplace chatter can be potentially devastating to productivity and the employees' general attitude. Gossip is typically viewed negatively because it brings falsehoods, rumors, and slanderous statements into the workplace and often causes conflicts in relationships.

I get hundreds of bits of information through emails, texts, phone calls, and conversation. Almost all of it goes in one ear and out the other unless I hear it from proven reliable sources or have seen the described offenses with my own eyes. Otherwise, I don't believe it and choose not to let it occupy my mind. It's just gossip; it serves no purpose except for some form of sick entertainment.

The workplace is a perfect brewery for gossip. A group of people—often the same ones every day—who are confined to small workspaces breed familiarity and often have intimate knowledge of each other's personal lives. Many people frequently crave negative and sensational information, while jealousy and dislike for others often serve as roots for gossip.

Because leaders are usually in the position to make decisions about many things, including disputes and allegations, it becomes especially important that you do not jump to conclusions based on hearsay. We must not believe every bit of gossip we hear, and if it appears to be something important, then we need to investigate and verify before making an accusation.

Recall President Ronald Reagan's quote regarding nuclear disarmament with the Russians: "Trust but verify." This phrase comes from the Russian proverb "*Doveryai no proveryai*," which means the same thing.

THE CONSEQUENCES OF GOSSIP

Besides hurt feelings and damaged reputations, there are plenty of adverse consequences when gossip runs amok at the workplace.

Productivity slows down because people are too busy minding other people's business. They may be too engaged in talking about others or listening intently about someone else's misfortunes. They are simply too busy gossiping to work.

Trust in leadership and in coworkers is often eroded as a result of gossip. People expect their leaders or managers to create a hostility-free work environment. They don't understand why leadership would allow trash-talking and don't understand how their coworkers can say such nasty things about them or other people. They will often take sides, perhaps with coworkers against another group of coworkers or against management and leadership. It creates division and can leak into the rest of the workplace, creating a hostile environment. This, again, decimates productivity, quality, and trust.

Gossip may affect the mental and spiritual health of your workers. Anxiety may increase among your employees as rumors circulate. It can also make facts less trusted; without any clear information and a trusted way to know what is factual and what is not, confusion and chaos will result. Anxiety causes stress, sleep disorders, high blood pressure, and even eating disorders, which can all lead to mental illness, such as depression, and which can even make people physically ill. This means a loss of work time and lost productivity.

WAYS TO DEAL WITH GOSSIP

There are plenty of strategies to deal with gossip in the workplace or anywhere else. I have used plenty of different approaches because gossip is always a problem in the workplace; however, the following points are borrowed from Marcel Schwantes's *Leadership from the Core*,[1] which offers a repertoire of tactics that can be highly effective.

1. **Enact "zero-tolerance" policies on workplace gossip.** Many companies protect employees from disclosing sensitive information to others. If, for example, a manager discloses confidential information that leads to workplace gossip about an employee, that manager faces the risk of disciplinary action or even job termination. The problem with this policy is that it is difficult to enforce. I have always had issues with people disclosing their salaries. Even high-level professionals discuss their salaries and benefits, which often causes myriad issues.

2. **Set an example.** Be a good role model for others to follow and don't engage in gossip. Be assertive, walk away, or change the subject when the gossip starts. The message you're communicating to others is that the behavior won't be tolerated.

3. **Let the boss know.** Have the courage to inform your immediate boss if the gossip is growing and gaining followers. Management that supports a healthy work environment should now address the issue in a way that reinforces and promotes a positive culture.

4. **Address the perpetrators.** This will take some courage, but stand up to the lead perpetrators and address them one-on-one in a neutral and more private room or office so others can't overhear. The point is not a pummel session, but to tactfully demonstrate with specific examples how your colleague's behavior is affecting and disrupting work.

5. **If you're a manager/leader, meet with your team.** Bring up the topic of gossip in a staff meeting to educate your team on its negative consequences. Perhaps the people involved in the gossip are unaware of the consequences.

6. **Encourage positive gossip.** The flip side of negative gossip is to create a culture where people share positive stories about work, customers, and culture. Think of examples where peers and bosses can communicate to one another what they feel proud about at work. An example would be an employee going above and beyond in serving a customer, then management

sharing the story company-wide and through social media to increase brand value. Start morning huddles with positive gossip and reinforce the cultural values and key behaviors you want through storytelling.

7. **Ignore the gossiper.** Gossipmongers thrive on attention and will prey on open and inviting ears. Your course of action is to be busy and preoccupied with your work (as you should be) so you're not available to listen. When the gossiper hands off the juicy gossip baton to you (because they want to spread it by enlisting other gossipers), don't take it.

8. **Turn it back on the gossiper with a positive thing to say.** Deflect the negative gossip with the exact opposite, by saying something refreshingly positive that you perceive to be true and fair—the other side of the coin. A complimentary remark about the person being attacked will stop the gossiper in their tracks. You may not see them visit you again. This may be a way to discourage future, unwanted visits.

9. **Keep your private life private.** Unless you have absolute certainty that you can trust a coworker, the rule of thumb is plain and simple: Don't trust personal information with anyone at work that will be fodder for gossip. The dead giveaway that you're dealing with serial gossipers is this: If you find them gossiping about others, you can bet that they will be gossiping about you as well. Don't give them ammunition to do so.

A great idiom to always practice that will help prevent many sad feelings, avoid conflicts, and prevent heartbreaks is the following that my dad used to preach to me whenever others would slander me because of my half-Asian ancestry: "Sticks and stones will break my bones, but words will never hurt me."

Food for thought

Don't believe everything you hear. You must always verify and get both sides of the story before making judgment or jumping to conclusions. Have you fallen into the "gossip trap" where you believe the gossip instead of seeking the truth by finding out both sides of the story?

CHAPTER 32

DON'T PROMOTE TO A LEVEL OF INCOMPETENCE

"In a hierarchy, every employee tends to rise to his level of incompetence."

—**Laurence J. Peter,** *The Peter Principle*

Bosses usually promote employees to higher levels of responsibility based on their superior work performance. Because some people are so good at their jobs, it stands to reason that they will succeed at higher levels of work, especially in leadership activities. This does not always work out according to expectations and may sometimes prove detrimental to the entire organizational structure—particularly to the promoted individual and definitely to the leader who has great expectations for the protégé.

Early in my leadership career, when my health clinic was relatively new, I decided to change the financial management structure from an outside accounting agency to hiring my own CFO. I had no idea what qualifications this position should have, so I hastily elevated a part-time staff bookkeeper to the position.

Debbie[1] had been with the company for about a year and was an excellent bookkeeper. She was great at her job and had never made a mistake, according to a reliable accountant who frequently reviewed her work for me. She could run circles around calculators and computers, according to this accountant. How could I not promote Debbie to become my CFO after hearing so many accolades and knowing her work was superior? She would become my partner to help grow this clinic.

I quickly gave her a generous salary and full-time benefits, sent her to a few finance seminars, and gave her as much time as she needed with the consulting accountant to learn her job. I even had plans to send her back to college so she could work on an accounting degree. I had been satisfied to see my leadership was creating a top-notch CFO from the ground up. She and the accounting department were going to be my Taj Mahal—a masterpiece. Debbie, in the meantime, was on cloud nine, as she knew she made it to the top!

But my Taj Mahal was crumbling and sinking faster than the *Titanic* after only three months. It was obvious Debbie was in way over her head. She was supposed to meet with my board's finance committee every month; that never happened. She was supposed to have created an inventory system for our increasing assets; she didn't even get started. She was supposed to develop an internal finance department supported by a payroll clerk, an accounts payable clerk, and an accounts receivable clerk; that never got going. In fact, everything I asked her to do just didn't get done. She had excuses for everything. Meanwhile, our accounting program was in dire straits, and I soon had to bring back the outside accounting agency to get it on track again. Instead of the Taj Mahal, I had created Frankenstein's monster! I fired her not long after I discovered she failed to pay the state and federal payroll taxes for two months in a row. It wasn't that we didn't have the money to pay for it; she just didn't do it.

The ultimate kicker to this experience was that two years later, I read in the local papers that Debbie was arrested for defrauding a local business of hundreds of thousands of dollars through cooked-up bookkeeping activities. I had dodged a bullet, and I had learned an important lesson.

THE PETER PRINCIPLE

The Peter Principle was originally written in 1969 by Dr. Laurence J. Peter and Dr. Raymond Hull[2] and was intended to be a work of satire. The principle, however, rang so true in hierarchical organizations that it became a popular topic to address at many corporate meetings. The principle simply explains that a person who has a high level of competency at a job will eventually earn a promotion to a higher or more senior level, typically requiring a different skill set. If this promoted individual who acquires this new skill set succeeds, they continue to be promoted until they reach a level they cannot succeed at. This is called *promoting to a level of incompetence*. These people may eventually get terminated from the job due to their failure to rise to the level of their new position, they may get demoted, or they may become stuck at this final level—called the *final placement* or *Peter's plateau* in the book. This leads to Peter's corollary: "In time, every post tends to be occupied by an employee who is incompetent to carry out its duties."

"The Peter Principle: A Theory of Decline" by Edward P. Lazear[3] attempts to discredit the principle by indicating that people typically get promoted because they have met the standards to do the job; therefore, they should be capable and are promoted to those higher positions. Lazear explains that some are able to meet the expectations of the new job once they are in, while others cannot and fail. Lazear argues that this is a function of mere statistics, rather than criteria.

Since most companies have built in a sort of regression of performance for the position, once individuals are promoted, the company expects a lower performance to avoid complete failure. Many firms inflate the promotion criterion and the standards of the position (the job expectations) to offset the Peter principle. The more important the transitory component is (for instance, going from a support clerk to the manager of a unit) relative to total variation in ability (the skill set differences between a clerk and manager), the larger the amount that the standard is inflated (the job description of the manager becomes more in-depth than it really should be to get the potential manager as close to the job requirements as possible). This same logic applies to other situations. It explains why movie sequels are worse than the original film and why second visits to restaurants are less rewarding than the first. The expectations for the movie sequel are greater (the standards are inflated): "I can't wait 'til the sequel comes out. It'll be as good as the original." Often, the sequel fails to live up to those expectations because they were too inflated.

WHY PROMOTE TO A LEVEL OF INCOMPETENCE?

Probably the simplest reason a worker would be promoted to a level of incompetence is that good leaders are difficult to find and train. So when a person excels at a lower-functioning job, they are suddenly deemed a star. They are pegged to be the person who is going to help lead others and make the leader's job easier, get the workers to work more efficiently, and be effectively productive. It's as if we are desperate and act too quickly to promote this individual to a position of higher responsibility. We often do not even give them the tools, such as training or education, to succeed. It's a quick fix for filling up leadership spots.

There are times that I have promoted employees to a higher and more responsible position based on my observations of their intellect, work ethic, and ability to think outside the box. Their job performance at their current job may not have been all that great, but I saw potential. I believed in them and wanted to give them a chance. However, this often went south too, primarily because I didn't invest the time to train and educate them, thinking they were so smart and skilled that they already had the ability to do the job or were smart enough to catch on quickly without any formal training.

A well-known study[4] reviewed the performance of 53,035 sales employees at 214 American companies from 2005 to 2011. During this time, 1,531 of those sales reps were promoted to become sales managers. The data revealed that the best salespeople were more likely to be promoted but were also more likely to perform poorly as managers.

"Consistent with the Peter principle, we find that promotion decisions place more weight on current performance than would be justified if firms only tried to promote the best potential managers," the researchers concluded.

"The most productive worker is not always the best candidate for manager, and yet firms are significantly more likely to promote top frontline sales workers into managerial positions. As a result, the performance of a new manager's subordinates declines relatively more after the managerial position is filled by someone who was a strong salesperson prior to promotion."

In this case, each company relied too heavily on sales as a criterion for promotion, paying twice for the mistake. Removing a high-performing sales associate from the line potentially upsets her client relationships and puts the revenue of those accounts in jeopardy. The team, newly under her direction, is at greater risk of underperforming as she struggles in a role that demands quite different abilities. "These findings underscore the possibility that promoting based on lower-level job skills rather than managerial skills can be extremely costly," the professors opined.

Dr. Alan Benson, one of the coauthors of the research, was surprised. "I expected that the best salespeople would become merely good managers: Some skills translate to management, and others don't," he said. "To see that the best salespeople were becoming the worst sales managers was surprising."

The authors can't say how often companies stumble into the Peter principle and how often they embrace it. Some firms may promote great salespeople "to encourage workers to exert effort in their current job roles and to maintain norms of fairness," they speculated. Counting sales is easily compared to "other, more subjective or fungible employee characteristics in promotion decisions." This new information, Dr. Benson said, "suggests firms were willing to lower the bar to promote the best salespeople."

THE CONSEQUENCES FOR THE LEADERS AND THE PROMOTED

Disappointment is the primary consequence for both leaders and the promoted. Leaders desperately want the promoted individual to succeed. In part, that desire is about how a leader's legacy will carry on, but importantly, under a good leader's tutelage, the promoted can take on many of the responsibilities that the leader or another manager formerly held, and can help make the leader's life more peaceful and more creatively productive. When things go wrong for the promoted, the leader begins to second-guess themselves about their ability to judge people and may lose the self-confidence to make decisions about other crucial situations in the future.

The promoted individual is also faced with disappointment. At first, the promotion elevated their status, and it made them feel good to be recognized for their hard work. It also gave them hope for financial success and prestige. But if the promoted eventually gets fired because of poor performance, it could destroy their self-esteem, happiness, and contentment. The promoted may second-guess themselves as well, wondering if perhaps they are not as good as they were told.

From both perspectives, the damage is extensive, including productivity decline, stress, and tension for both the leader and the promoted.

AVOID A PROMOTED EMPLOYEE PETERING OUT

After many years of mistakes—and I still make them—the best advice I can give about promoting good workers is to make sure there is a mutual understanding about expectations. What does the leader expect? And, just as important, what does the promoted expect? This is why job descriptions are so critical. They must be used as guides, as well as the evaluation criteria for job performances. The job description becomes the road map for everyone's success. Once the expectations are all on the table, you must invest in training and educating the promoted for as long as it takes—within reason, of course. Additionally, supporting the promoted individual through educational seminars and one-on-one training is advantageous for boosting their confidence in the new position.

Ironically, a sure way to avoid the Peter principle is to avoid promoting anyone. Of course, that's impossible, but you can focus on promoting those who have the skills of the new position rather than the old one. Those employees who have a considerable dose of self-awareness may know that management, for all its perks, might not be worth the burden it will impose on the promoted.

My dad had an army buddy who was a great first sergeant. He was good at every job the commanding officers gave him, so eventually, they had him go to officer candidate school to become an officer. He graduated at the top of his class and became my dad's boss, but he was awful. He made mistakes and was always disorganized. He couldn't get his assigned work done. Soon, he volunteered to go back to his rank of first sergeant with a reduction of pay. He later told my dad that he just wasn't cut out to be an officer and he should have stayed put where he excelled.

Finally, employees are an important and costly commodity for any business. Without solid employees and leaders in the right jobs, a business will ultimately fail. Avoid the Peter principle, but if you insist on implementing it, make sure the sequel is a good one.

Food for thought

Avoid promoting anyone to a level of incompetence. It isn't fair to the promoted, to the business, to the customers or clients, and definitely not to the leader. Promote carefully and systematically with close monitoring and support. Have you ever promoted anyone to a higher level hoping they could do the job but knowing they probably couldn't? Have you ever been promoted to a level of incompetence?

CHAPTER 33

DON'T BE A STRANGER

"Know thyself."

—Greek aphorism

Do you know who you are? This is not a trick question but a contemplative one. Have you ever taken a few minutes to wonder, "Who am I? What am I all about? What is my purpose?"

As I headed toward adolescence during the mid-1960s, hippies and flower children asked, "Hey, man, why are we here?" Of course, it was never clear whether these young "model citizens" were on acid trips or if they were just philosophically superior to everyone else.

In Michael Singer's book *The Surrender Experiment*, I stumbled on the answer to the hippies' question. He explains that we have no control over the fate of our lives and that the flow of life around us did not begin when we were born, and it won't end when we die. Singer goes on to explain that what manifests in front of us is truly extraordinary, that everything is the result of all the cosmic forces that have been interacting together for billions of years. We have no control over what we want or what we think about the way things should be, because we are merely characters in a long-playing drama called life. It is the natural result of the forces of creation. (No, I don't think this guy is crazy!)

So does it matter if the hippies know who they are, what they are, or where they are going? Even though the book suggests that our life's destiny is a matter of fate, we still have control over our individual lives as it relates to daily activities, how we conduct ourselves, how we make decisions, how we dream, and all the other events of daily life. It is important to know who we are, especially if we are leaders; in order to lead, we do need to have a good grip on our values and beliefs. How and why you are who you are will determine how people follow you. It can be difficult for them to understand what we want and how they should act within the organization—especially if we have no sense of what makes us tick.

TO BE OR TO DO?

A good place to start the exercise of figuring out who we are is to ask the question "What to be or what to do?" Children are frequently asked what they want to *be* when they grow up rather than what they want to *do*. When I asked my son, Adam, who was four at the time, what he wanted to be, he couldn't decide whether to be Superman or Spider-Man. When I asked what he wanted to *do*, he replied, "I want to fly around and beat up bad guys." A couple of weeks later, he wanted to be Batman. He didn't ever really know what he wanted to *be*, but he always knew what he wanted to *do*.

A good leader can see what they want to do with a project, organization, or process. A way to know yourself better is to know what you want to do and not necessarily what you want to be. As leaders, we must know who we are. Over many years of practicing self-awareness and trying to figure out who I am and what I do, I have come up with some strategies that may help you understand yourself better.

WRITE A PERSONAL MISSION STATEMENT

An excellent way to discover yourself is to write a personal mission statement. I first came across this concept years ago when I read a book by Stephen Covey titled *First Things First.* I read it cover to cover three times. It is earmarked, labeled, written on, smudged, stained, and torn in some parts. Before this, I thought only businesses and companies wrote mission statements. Why shouldn't we, as individuals, have our own?

I wanted to know more about myself, so I did some self-contemplative exercises and wrote my own mission statement based on Covey's guidelines. If done right, a personal mission statement can become your beacon of light, the compass that guides your purpose. Of course, this mission statement may change over time. I wrote my first one when I was in my early 40s, and it was an entire page long. It has undergone several transformations, and now, it is simple and portable; I can recite it anytime from memory.

KEEP A DAILY JOURNAL

Another great strategy to help you learn about yourself is through self-reflection. I have learned so much about myself through daily writing. I've come to understand my moods, eccentricities, and how to become a nicer person through self-control. It helped me recognize how to act and speak to others more respectfully when reviewing my actions for that day.

A journal can be organized in any number of ways, and you don't even have to write daily. There are no rules. Just write whenever, wherever, and whatever. Put memorabilia in it too, like travel postcards, airline napkins, and notes from people. It's fun to look back and reminisce, and you might relearn something you forgot or see something you missed.

PRACTICE YOGA, MEDITATION, TAI CHI, AND MINDFULNESS

Mindfulness, meditation, and disciplines like yoga and tai chi help you form connections between body, mind, and spirit. You can learn a lot about yourself by clearing your mind and letting your heart and spiritual being take over.

There are numerous articles and videos that describe the health benefits of these ancient practices. To incorporate this strategy into everyday life would certainly help improve your self-awareness and self-regulation—two key components of emotional intelligence that can help leadership and life skills.

WRITE YOUR OWN OBITUARY OR EPITAPH

It's a bit morbid, I know, but wouldn't you want a say on how your obituary would read? This is a good exercise on self-awareness through deep introspection and is much like writing your own personal mission statement. How do you want people to remember you?

An epitaph is interesting. You're limited to a few words to describe a person's entire life. I once read an epitaph written on a headstone of a 17-year-old boy who died in the 1600s in Charleston, South Carolina. I don't recall the exact words, but in part, it went something like this:

He died saving another's life.

These few words instantly conjure up an image of the boy—dependable, caring, honest, with no regard for his own personal safety for the sake of helping others.

Ask yourself how people will remember you or how you want to be remembered.

USE MIRRORS—PHYSICAL AND SOCIAL

Mirrors are natural feedback gadgets. They reflect what you look like at that moment. You can then act based on this visual feedback: a pimple here, missed shaving a corner there, puffy eyes after eating too much sushi soaked in soy sauce, hair out of place. They help pinpoint your flaws and insecurities to target what you need to improve about yourself.

Social mirrors tend to be mostly auditory feedbacks. Friends, loved ones, and even enemies tell you what they think about you or what you should be doing and how you should do it. There is certainly no shortage of opinions, and they can be valuable if you listen and take appropriate action. You don't have to believe or act on every suggestion and opinion, but just make sure it doesn't go in one ear and out the other.

EMBRACE FAME

As mentioned in earlier chapters, the most important tool to help us learn about ourselves is through experiences of failure, adversity, mistakes, and enemies. FAME is what brings color to your life, even excitement. They are the difficult activities you want and need to learn from—even cope with—through daily journaling, writing your obit or epitaph, meditation, and mirrors.

This is why we need to know who we are. If we are in touch with ourselves, we can deal with and learn from FAME. This is what will help make us great leaders and why we don't want to be a stranger to ourselves.

Food for thought

You must know yourself in order to be a great leader and have a wonderful life!

CHAPTER 34

DON'T KNOW MUCH

"Ignorance is bliss."

—**Anonymous**

Originally composed by Lou Adler and Herb Alpert and later modified by Sam Cooke, the song "Wonderful World" is about how knowledge and education cannot dictate feelings, but the feeling of love can make the world a wonderful place to live.

This idea fits well with the concept that good leadership is not always about being a brilliant and studious person with lots of knowledge or education. The greatest leaders in history were not always the best students, but they all possessed a deep sense of passion, heart, vision, and love. Many exhibited kindness, respect, and forgiveness toward others.

Albert Einstein dropped out of high school at 15, Henry Ford did so at 16, Bill Gates left Harvard in his junior year, and Thomas Edison dropped out after a few months of formal schooling because he had difficulty paying attention. This list goes on and on. Walt Disney, one of the pioneers of entertainment and animation, made very poor grades and dropped out of school at 15. Richard Branson was also a high school dropout. All these people were remarkably successful. They changed the world in so many ways because they had an intense passion and desire to pursue their dreams.

CROCS AND GATORS

My oldest daughter, Erin, was 10 when I took her to Florida for the first time. She was a precocious child, declaring her desire to become an animal rights activist when she was only two! By second grade, she knew the taxonomy of most wildlife animals and was an expert on *Canis lupus* (wolves, for those of you who are not familiar with Latin names).

As the plane descended toward a Florida airport, I pointed at the countryside below and teasingly exclaimed, "Look at those crocodiles, Erin!" She quickly glanced out the window, then immediately rebuked, "Daddy, crocodiles are not indigenous to North America. Only alligators are."

A bit stunned at the patronizing remark from a 10-year-old, I wasn't sure what to say. I never really knew the difference between these two ugly creatures, nor did I really care, so I simply replied, "Okay . . . um . . . Well, you know Daddy's a biologist, don't you?"

She swiftly retorted, "You didn't learn much in biology school, so how did you become the boss of your company?"

I was speechless. I didn't know how to respond at that moment, so I just smiled and thought about that question. She had related two events as if they were connected, the implication being that I am not a good student, at least in biology, so how did I manage to become a boss—a leader of my business?

After months—even years—of contemplation, I recognized that the reason I became the boss of my company is because I had a deep passion for helping underprivileged, underinsured, and uninsured people get better access to health care. I found it to be a challenge and rewarding. I gave it my all. I put my time, love, care, gratitude, and emotional intelligence into building a top health center to help the poor because that is what I truly believed in. It wasn't necessarily because I was smart that I became the boss of my health center; I was successful at surrounding myself with very smart and knowledgeable people who knew things that I didn't. I had heart, vision, and the love to make this work, and the emotional intelligence carried me on to success.

It took a while, but I finally concluded that I didn't need to be smart in biology to be a successful boss. They were unrelated skill sets.

SMART SUCCESS

What does it mean to be smart? In many developed countries, smartness is defined by how well we perform in school. But being smart does not always result in success, as is evidenced by my previous story.

When I was in grade school and high school, I was always intrigued by kids who were smart, because I wanted to be one of them. In high school, social maturity has a lot to do with what groups we fit into. These groups would often dictate how we acted and how we thought about others. For example, the "popular" groups were usually made up of athletes, cheerleaders, the good-looking kids, and those who came from affluent families. There were also groups made up of misfits—the smokers, the drug users, and those who got into fights a lot. These were the "bad" kids.

The toughest group to get into and usually the smallest group was the smart kids. You could only get in if you were a top student. Even though the smart group didn't have to be from rich families, they were frequently labeled as arrogant, standoffish, and too good to associate with others. But they weren't successful otherwise. Most didn't have other friends, they didn't have jobs, they didn't go out on dates, and they didn't do much of anything other than study. They were smart but not well rounded.

In high school, I had the good fortune to enroll in an advanced chemistry course with a teacher named Mr. Hodge. In his class, I learned about being competitive. He always wrote a percentage grade on our test papers, but he also included our rank as compared with our classmates. I hated losing, so I studied hard for his exams and usually finished close to the top of my classes—but not always the number one! So, was I really smart in chemistry, or was it my competitive nature and burning desire not to lose?

In college, I took a Latin class with Dr. Swift, the chair of the department at the time. Latin and languages have always come easy to me, so I skipped a lot of classes and only showed up for exams. He was miffed at me, but I didn't care, because I aced all the exams. The policy in the class was that if you had an A going into the finals, you were exempt from taking the final exam. He excluded me from that list, and when I went to him after class to ask about it, he became angry with me and exclaimed, "All you premeds are the same. You're just interested in the grade and not learning!" He did finally relent and exempted me from the finals after I threatened to go to the ombudsman. I was smart in Latin, but my attitude sucked, and I failed as a good and responsible student. I did not practice good emotional intelligence.

As I got older and entered medical school, I realized those who always made the top grades on exams were not always the best clinically or personally. Some patients didn't like them because they spoke over the patients' heads and were unable to simply relate to people. Their bedside manner was awkward. Their presentation of patient information to our attending physicians was subpar too. If they were so smart, then why couldn't they relate to others? How could they become successful doctors if they couldn't even relate to people?

The paradox of using school performance as an indicator of success is that we all know people who appear to *not* have a lot of knowledge but who do extremely well on standardized exams and become successful in later life. For example, Albert Einstein purportedly failed basic arithmetic classes in grade school. Conversely, there are those who seem to know everything about anything but do poorly on exams.

What does this observation mean? I'm not sure, but as it relates to leadership, I believe that smartness, when defined by educational performances, test scores, and IQ levels, means very little. Great leaders are great because they are visionaries, can see the big picture, and are experts at motivating and managing people.

THE FOREST FOR THE TREES

An important discovery I have made over many years of being a leader and always looking for leaders to fill a variety of roles is that some people are very good at knowing every minute detail but they miss the bigger picture. They can't see the forest for the trees, as the saying goes. They don't know what the forest looks like and how it relates to its environment, but they can tell you every detail about a specific tree. They are superb problem solvers, but they don't know how the solutions lead to bigger goals.

In my profession as a physician and a health-care executive, I know many doctors who are extraordinarily brilliant. Getting accepted into medical school is a difficult process and depends largely on performance during the undergraduate curriculum, especially in the sciences. Most medical schools have a set of metrics, including high grades and exceptionally high scores on medical entrance exams. But they typically don't assess emotional intelligence well.

Many times, these kids do get accepted because their academic performance is so over the top that the interviewers begin drooling. But they don't ever make the best doctors. I call them tree people. They ultimately become experts of miniscule information, such as knowing every detail of the human body. They can recite the entire Krebs cycle in detail, but many cannot verbalize its purpose (which is cellular respiration).

A good leader does not need to or want to know everything. They don't have to be the smartest in the group; they need to see the forest.

A leader can surround themselves with tree people, but they have to be able to put all those trees together to see the forest.

Food for thought

If you are a leader, you don't want or need to be the smartest person on your team. Your role is to create a team of smart people who know a lot about the details. Your job is to see the big picture. Surround yourself with "tree" people who can give you expert information surrounding a problem or issue, but you have to be able to put it together. Check yourself. If you are the leader of your group or organization, are you the smartest person? Do you think you should be?

CHAPTER 35

DON'T BE A TWO-DIMENSIONAL SPACE ALIEN

"Being normal is boring."

—Marilyn Monroe

To become a board-certified physician executive, I was required to spend an entire week in Tampa, Florida, and to attend a conference listening to esoteric presentations related to being an executive. One of the lectures was focused on the importance of dressing to look like an executive. After all, they stressed, first impressions open doors for further opportunities.

It occurred to me that not only should we look our spiffiest when playing the role of a leader but also, more importantly, that our behavior, personality, and conduct are even more essential displays of a top leader. These characteristics are often the initial details others use to make judgments about our leadership. Like high-profile personalities, such as actors and politicians, leaders are constantly scrutinized and under the social microscope. People want to know everything about you, they want to know what makes you tick, and they want to know how to maneuver themselves to be on your good side.

I have learned that the best persona to possess as a leader is your own: Just be yourself. Part of the reason some of us attain leadership is our positive and strong personalities. Masquerading other personality traits just doesn't work; stereotypical boss characteristics, such as toughness, barking orders, and being arrogant, are more harmful than effective. There is no need to masquerade as a leader when you actually are the leader.

Over many years of leadership, I have found three primary personality characteristics that leaders should avoid: trying to be someone they are not, working really hard to be a serious and straitlaced executive type, and being a dull and gloomy leader. The following segments describe each.

SPACEMEN

When I was a kid, I loved watching and reading science fiction movies and novels. The fantasy of life on other planets and imagining what it's like in other worlds were too irresistible for an imaginative boy like me.

The trouble was that most alien beings in movies and books at the time were stereotyped as superior in intellect and strength. But all these out-of-world beings were blah, boring, and ugly! In the movies, when the aliens visited earthlings, they just wanted to be taken to our leaders and then wanted to conquer our planet. They were never fun at all!

Take the robot Gort from the movie *The Day the Earth Stood Still.* How boring was he? He just stood there for days in front of the flying saucer ship—no talking, dancing, or singing. His master, Klaatu, was just as bad. He was the prototypical two-dimensional space alien.

Leaders should be human and not act like a two-dimensional space alien. They don't have to wear a suit and tie every day or bark orders at everyone. Let others see the real you. Avoid obsessing about being the smartest, the best, or the know-it-all. Have depth in your character that includes who you really are. Show passion, caring, compassion, and love of life. People are more apt to respect and understand you better than if you are a two-dimensional space alien. Have *joie de vivre*—the joy of life!

MASQUERADING

We have all fantasized about being someone else. Halloween masquerade parties are popular because they allow us to be someone different—our alter ego, perhaps. Wasn't it fun to fantasize about being someone famous or a powerful action figure when we were kids? It's still fun to pretend.

Once, around the age of five, I wanted to be Popeye, so I ate cans of spinach just like the cartoon character. I got so sick that I spent the rest of the day at the toilet instead of growing bigger biceps. Another time, despite having 20/20 vision, I wanted to wear eyeglasses so I could be like Clark Kent. I thought it would be so cool to look like a nerd but be able to instantly turn into Superman. It did not work.

The troubling thing about being someone you're not is that we soon lose credibility. People will lose respect for you and your position if you are inauthentic. Remember Senator Marco Rubio during the 2016 presidential debates? At one event, he suddenly went on the attack. He tried to be like Donald Trump by using quips and name-calling to degrade Trump's character.[1] I believe Mr. Rubio's aggressive personality change to imitate Mr. Trump backfired and made him look bad, reducing his credibility with voters. Attempting to change who you are for perceived gain is transparent to others and rarely works.

When I was a third-year medical student, friends who were only a couple of years ahead of me and now newly minted medical interns suddenly pretended to not know me. They were rude and obstinate, ordering me and other third-year students around as if we were their personal slaves. They even made us call them *doctor*. I lost all respect for them.

GLOOMY GUS

I was standing in a short line at a base camp shop on Lone Mountain, Montana, waiting to purchase zip-lining tickets when an excited mother accompanied by her two teenage daughters started to raise her voice. There were several time options for the zip-lining excursions. The mom kept asking if the girls wanted to go on the 10:00 or the 11:00 tour, but they maintained a dour, uninterested appearance and just kept shrugging. The mother, now tense and agitated, continued to raise her voice out of frustration and repeated the question. After a few seconds of silence, one of the girls, with a shrill voice and contorted facial gestures, screamed, "We just don't care, Mom! What*ever*!"

The salesclerk, a teenage boy of about 18 or 19, watched the exchange and remarked in a deadpan voice, "Wow, real Debbie Downers, right?"

The mom took a deep breath, smiled, and apologized to the boy, then said, "Let's go, girls. We'll regroup. Think of something you really want to do, and I'll make it happen!" The girls giggled and followed their mom with renewed energy and excitement.

Attitudes and perspectives are difficult to manage. They often reflect a person's values, desires, goals, and—most importantly—their past histories and experiences. Certainly, biology and genetics play a role in how we view things. But what about the leader's influence on attitudes and perspectives? Why were the girls' manners so seemingly poor? Was it just their adolescent nature? Were they afraid of heights and really did not want to zip-line? Maybe the mom was making them do it. Were they up all night and were simply just tired? Or was their Debbie Downer demeanor a reflection of the leader—the mom? How did she initially sell the activity to her daughters? Perhaps she said, "I don't care if you don't want to; you are going to go zip-lining, and you're going to have fun. Do it or else!"

The story has a good ending, because the mom used her parenting leadership skills and relented to the girls' wants, and everyone became happy about it, except maybe the teenage salesclerk.

THE SAGE AND THE SPIDER— AN ANCIENT STORY FROM INDIA

A sage went to bathe in a river one day and spied a poisonous spider struggling in the water. He cupped it with both hands and carried it to the riverbank. As he let the spider go, it stung him.

The same thing happened the next day.

The man repeated his kindness on the third day, with the same scenario. The spider finally asked, "Why do you keep saving me? You know I will sting you every time because that is what I do."

The sage replied, "And this is what I do," as he gently placed the spider along the embankment.

It is so important to be yourself in everything you do, especially in leadership. There is no need to take the persona of some stereotypical character; you don't need to act vengeful or tough, or be mean and decisive, just because now you are the leader and supposed to exhibit those traits. People will peg you as a phony and will lose all respect for you. Be what you are and do what you do. Add a bit of optimism and positive attitude if you don't already have them. With integrity and believability, people will follow you.

Food for thought

Be yourself when you are a leader. Your abilities and personality are what made you the leader, so there is no need to masquerade with a false identity. Do you try to be someone you're not?

CHAPTER 36

DON'T BE A MANAGER WHEN YOU ARE SUPPOSED TO BE A LEADER

"Management is doing things right.
Leadership is doing the right things."
—Peter Drucker

Many people are confused by the terms *manager* and *leader*. A manager works within a system of rules, whereas a leader works on creating the system. The CEO of an organization is the visionary and determines the company's direction. The manager makes sure tasks are accomplished according to the rules and plans in place created by the leader.

This is often a tricky notion. For example, remember Debbie, the CFO mentioned in Chapter 32? I once viewed her as a leader. She had a two-year accounting degree and was basically an accountant, but she was not really a leader. She had no training or experience in making high-level decisions. So I tried to make her into a leader by attempting to have her get her four-year degree, as well as sending her to continuing education courses. I spent over a year on this project, but she simply was not a leader. She was a manager.

Titles do not make someone into a leader. Leaders are guiders, innovators, imaginers—someone who can see the future. A leader is able to put many pieces of information together to obtain that vision. This is an important concept for people to get: Not everyone is a leader!

Food for thought

Leaders work on the system, and managers work within a system! Don't confuse the two! Are you a leader or manager?

CHAPTER 37

DOS FROM DON'TS

Over a lifetime of failure, adversity, mistakes, and enemies, I have learned many lessons about what not to do. My personal mission statement noted below is a list of the positive lessons I have learned from many of the don'ts.

Be kind, do good, give generously.
Respect all and love unconditionally.

Always take the high road and
rise above in all matters.
The world is small, so don't burn bridges.

Smile often and frown less.
Speak less and hear more.

Stay anchored, but
Dream boldly and dare to adventure!

Dance, play, and love with boundless gusto!

Seize the good of life; do what you love,
and love what you do.

Cherish yesterday, dream tomorrow,
and love today.

After all, it is not how long you live;
it's how well you lived.

NOTES

CHAPTER 1

1. https://en.wikipedia.org/wiki/Buckminster_Fuller
2. https://medium.com/@penguinpress/an-excerpt-from-how-not-to-be-wrong-by-jordan-ellenberg-664e708cfc3d
3. During World War II, the United States commissioned a select group of mathematicians that came to be known as the Statistical Research Group (SRG), based out of Columbia University.
4. Wald was asked to make assumptions on incomplete and partial data since he did not have the bullet hole statistics of the airplanes that did not come back. This is called statistical bias in the world of statisticians.
5. https://knowledge.wharton.upenn.edu/article/can-creativity-be-taught
6. Ibid.
7. Ibid.
8. John Denver, *Country Boy*, PBS video, 2015.
9. https://en.wikipedia.org/wiki/Pareidolia
10. https://brandongaille.com/7-thinking-outside-the-box-examples
11. https://er.jsc.nasa.gov/seh/ricetalk.htm

CHAPTER 2

1. The term *shikata ga nai* was used commonly in the 1940s, but modern and practical use of the word is now *sho ga nai*.

CHAPTER 3

1. https://www.nba.com/history/legends/profiles/bill-russell
2. https://www.snopes.com/fact-check/abraham-lincoln-failure

CHAPTER 6

1. https://www.facebook.com/JIBusinessEthics/

CHAPTER 7

1. *New York Post*, Saturday, October 26, 2019.
2. https://en.wikipedia.org/wiki/Buck_passing
3. T. G. Shields and R. K. Goidel, "Taking Credit and Avoiding Blame: Good News, Spin Control, and Democratic Accountability," *Political Communication* 15, no. 1 (1998): 99–115, 10.1080/10584609.1998.11641157
4. https://www.ncbi.nlm.nih.gov/pmc/articles/PMC6405044/
5. https://www.researchgate.net/publication/225822507_Apologies_and_Transformational_Leadership

CHAPTER 9

1. Tale of Two Diseases, https://www.butterfliesandhope.org/wp-content/uploads/2016/10/A-Tale-of-Two-Disease.pdf

CHAPTER 10

1. I read about this years ago in Stephen Covey's book *First Things First*.

CHAPTER 12

1. Laura Hillenbrand, *Unbroken: A World War II Story of Survival, Resilience, and Redemption* (New York: Random House, 2010).
2. https://apnews.com/article/2b700bf846494dd69d392a656c2f5f9a
3. Chris Wallace, *Countdown 1945: The Extraordinary Story of the Atomic Bomb and the 116 Days That Changed the World* (New York: Avid Reader Press, 2020).

CHAPTER 13

1. As told to me by Ahgri in July 2018.
2. https://www.healthline.com/health/first-impressions
3. https://www.gunsandammo.com/editorial/george-s-patton-guns-that-made-him-great/247778#:~:text=More%20than%20mere%20window%20dressing%2C%20General%20George%20S.,may%20have%20been%20the%20world%27s%20most%20powerful%20handguns
4. mph.neomed.edu/faculty-and-staff/faculty-list/ronald-dwinnells
5. Charlotte Hilton Andersen, "10 Unexpected Ways Your Clothes Can Change Your Mood," https://www.rd.com/list/clothes-affect-mood
6. "Enclothed Cognition," *Journal of Experimental Social Psychology* 48, no. 4 (July 2012).
7. https://www.willmarradio.com/big_country/morning_show/clothes-effect-mood/article_b713ee78-e5fb-11e5-a0e5-cb179616c352.html
8. https://www.greatschools.org/gk/articles/school-uniforms/

CHAPTER 14

1. https://www.definitions.net/definition/jamoke
2. https://www.merriam-webster.com/dictionary/jamoke
3. https://www.goodtherapy.org/blog/psychpedia/abstract-thinking
4. Laura Berk, *Exploring Lifespan Development*, 4th ed. (Hoboken, NJ: Pearson, 2017).
5. University of Kentucky, basic introductory psychology course, 1974.

CHAPTER 15

1. https://www.therecoveryvillage.com/mental-health/grief/related/grief-statistics/#:~:text=%20There%20are%20a%20few%20common%20causes%20of,it%20can%20cause%20both%20parties%20to...%20More%20
2. "Anne Hewlett Fuller, 87, Dies, Widow of Futurist Architect," *New York Times*, July 4, 1983, Section 1, p. 16.
3. https://www.theartstory.org/artist/fuller-buckminster/life-and-legacy
4. Lauren J. N. Brent et al., "The Neuroethology of Friendship," *Annals of the New York Academy of Sciences* 1316, no. 1 (May 2014): 1–17.
5. Ibid.

CHAPTER 16

1. From the Holy Bible: King James Version, Matthew 13:24–30, the Parable of the Tares.

CHAPTER 17

1. Daniel Levitin, *The Organized Mind: Thinking Straight in the Age of Information Overload* (New York: Dutton, 2014).
2. Pew Research Center analysis of the decennial Census 1960–2012; https://www.pewresearch.org/ft_dual-income-households-1960-2012-2
3. Ibid.
4. https://oureverydaylife.com/advantages-disadvantages-dualincome-families
5. *Wikipedia*, https://en.wikipedia.org/wiki/Two-front_war

CHAPTER 18

1. Computed tomography—an imaging device that combines X-rays using a computer, frequently referred to as CT or CAT scan.
2. Not his real name.
3. https://www.wisegeek.com/what-is-a-sawbones.htm#

CHAPTER 19

1. Dr. Kiljoy and Steve Fixit are fictional names.
2. https://insights.btoes.com/lean-resources/toyota-production-system-principles-introduction-to-tps
3. https://www.allaboutlean.com/jidoka-1/

CHAPTER 20

1. Pierro Ferrucci, *The Power of Kindness* (New York: Jeremy P. Tarcher, 2006).
2. Amy J. C. Cuddy, Matthew Kohut, and John Neffinger, "Connect, Then Lead," *Harvard Business Review*, July–August 2013.
3. https://www.forbes.com/sites/davidsturt/2018/10/24/how-purposeful-kindness-can-make-you-a-better-leader
4. https://www.ox.ac.uk/news/2016-10-05-being-kind-others-does-make-you-slightly-happier

5. Ibid.
6. https://www.ox.ac.uk/news/2016-10-05-being-kind-others-does-make-you-slightly-happier

CHAPTER 21

1. Not her real name.
2. Bill O'Reilly, *Killing England* (New York: Henry Holt, 2017).
3. "Japan's Shinzo Abe Leaves 'Abenomics' Project Unfinished," *Wall Street Journal*, August 28, 2020.
4. https://www.ccl.org/blog/4-components-good-health-enhance-leadership/

CHAPTER 23

1. https://www.americanprogress.org/issues/women/news/2018/08/06/454376/gender-matters/
2. Ibid.
3. Lara Stemple, JD, and Ilan H. Meyer, PhD, "The Sexual Victimization of Men in America: New Data Challenge Old Assumptions," *American Journal of Public Health*, published online, June 2014, doi: 10.2105/AJPH.2014.301946
4. Ibid.
5. Ibid.
6. https://www.psychologytoday.com/us/blog/media-spotlight/201505/when-men-face-sexual-harassment
7. https://www.brighthub.com/office/career-planning/articles/89649/#consequences-of-sexual-harassment-in-the-workplace
8. https://www.thebalancecareers.com/sexual-harassment-1918253

CHAPTER 24

1. https://mission-statement.com/nordstrom/
2. https://sharpencx.com/blog/nordstrom-customer-service
3. Ibid.
4. Ibid.

CHAPTER 25

1. https://www.healthline.com/health/parenting/helicopter-parenting
2. Gallup, *12: The Elements of Great Managing* (New York: Gallup Press, 2006).
3. Forbes Coaches Council, "Micromanaging? Here's How (and Why) You Should Stop," May 19, 2017, https://www.forbes.com/sites/forbescoachescouncil/2017/05/19/micromanaging-heres-how-and-why-you-should-stop/?sh=6849e89f7518
4. Dr. Venessa Marie Perry, Health Resource Solutions, LLC.
5. Karima Mariama-Arthur, Esq., WordSmithRapport.
6. Susanne Biro, Susanne Biro & Associates Coaching Inc.
7. Emily Kapit, ReFresh Your Step, LLC.
8. Alicia Reece, The Reece Group.
9. Alexandra Salamis, Integral Leadership Design.
10. Gia Ganesh, Gia Ganesh Coaching.
11. Suzi Pomerantz, Innovative Leadership International LLC.
12. Leila Bulling Towne, The Bulling Towne Group, LLC.
13. Aaron Levy, Raise The Bar Consulting.
14. Kelly Meerbott, You: Loud & Clear.
15. Ken Melrose Obituary, *Wall Street Journal*, May 16, 2020.

CHAPTER 26

1. Douglas Stone, Bruce Patton, and Sheila Heen, *Difficult Conversations: How to Discuss What Matters Most* (New York: Viking Penguin, 1999).
2. Ibid.

CHAPTER 28

1. https://www.verywellmind.com/evolution-anxiety-1392983
2. Joseph E. LeDoux, "Evolution of Human Emotion: A View through Fear," *Progress in Brain Research* 195 (2012): 431–442, doi:10.1016/B978-0-444-53860-4.00021-0
3. https://www.cdc.gov/vaccinesafety/ensuringsafety/history/index.html
4. https://www.cdc.gov/obesity/adult/causes.html
5. https://www.leadertoleader.org/fear-based-workplace-heather-hanson/

CHAPTER 29

1. Y. H. Huang et al., "Financial Decision-Makers' Views on Safety: What SH&E Professionals Should Know," *Professional Safety* (April 2009): 36–42.
2. https://www.osha.gov/dsg/InjuryIllnessPreventionProgramsWhitePaper.html
3. https://www.nsc.org/Portals/0/Documents/JSEWorkplaceDocuments/Journey-to-Safety-Excellence-Safety-Business-Case-Executives.pdf
4. Data provided by Sprout Wellness Solutions for ONE Health Ohio.

CHAPTER 30

1. Joel R. Davitz (ed.), *The Communication of Emotional Meaning* (New York: McGraw-Hill, 1964).
2. https://www.cnbc.com/2020/03/10/joe-biden-told-an-auto-worker-youre-full-of-shit-during-a-tense-argument-over-guns.html

CHAPTER 31

1. https://www.inc.com/marcel-schwantes/if-you-do-these-things-you-qualify-as-a-gossiper-which-research-says-can-ruin-yo.html

CHAPTER 32

1. Not her real name.
2. Laurence Peter and Raymond Hull, *The Peter Principle* (New York: William Morrow and Company, 1969).
3. Edward P. Lazear, "The Peter Principle: A Theory of Decline," The University of Chicago Press Journals, *Journal of Political Economy*, vol. 1, p. 21.
4. Alan Benson, Danielle Li, and Kelly Shue, "Promotions and the Peter Principle," *Quarterly Journal of Economics* 134, no. 4 (November 2019): 2085–2134; NBER Working Paper No. 24343 issued in February 2018. NBER Program(s):Corporate Finance, Labor Studies, https://www.nber.org/papers/w24343.

CHAPTER 35

1. https://www.nbcnews.com/politics/2016-election/shift-marco-rubio-attacks-donald-trump-name-ahead-debate-n525341

INDEX

A

B

E

F

N

O

P

R

S

T

U

V

ABOUT THE AUTHOR

Ronald Dwinnells, MD, MBA, is a pediatrician and a certified physician executive. He is the CEO of ONE Health Ohio, an integrated community health center program serving the medically uninsured, underinsured, and underserved populations in northeast Ohio. His clinics have served over one million patients during his 35 years at the helm.

He is also the founder and president of the Butterflies and Hope Memorial Foundation (www.butterfliesandhope.org), whose mission is to support and improve the lives of children, adolescents, and young people suffering from behavioral and mental health issues. He has authored and published several scholarly works on health-care delivery systems and is on the faculty of local universities, teaching topics on leadership, health-care delivery programs, health disparities, and physical diagnosis.

Dr. Dwinnells attributes his personal and professional growth and life's good fortunes to hard work, a good attitude, the love of life, and being raised in two cultures—Japanese and American. His extracurricular activities include mountain climbing (including Mt. Rainer, Fuji, Hood, St. Helens, Pikes Peak, Baker, Whitney, Shasta, Washington, and two continental high points of Mt. Kilimanjaro and Mt. Elbrus), running competitive road races, gardening, traveling, reading, creative writing, and exercising. He lives with his wife, Kathy; his daughters, Erin, Sarah, Emily, and Abbey; and his favorite (only) son, Adam, in Poland, Ohio.